KT-455-446

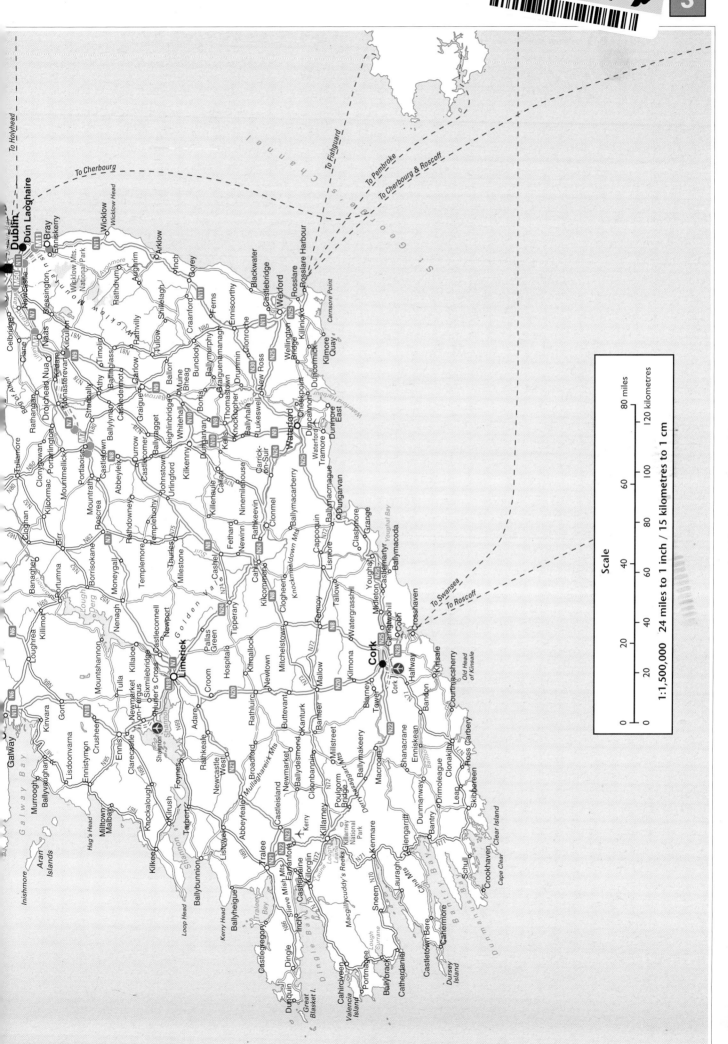

Scale

1:1,500,000   24 miles to 1 inch / 15 kilometres to 1 cm

0   20   40   60   80 miles

0   20   40   60   80   100   120 kilometres

PLACES OF INTEREST

ADARE *County Limerick* 28 A3
The pretty village of Adare, which once belonged to the Kildare Fitzgeralds, and then the Earls of Dunraven, has several items of interest. The Gothic Revival manor house, now a luxury hotel, was built by the 2nd Earl in 1832 to his own design with additional work by James Pain and A.W. Pugin. The main hall is defined by stone arches and a handsome rococo staircase while the ornamental gardens are splendid for strolling.
Medieval Desmond Castle, overlooking the River Maigue, still retains a fine square keep, as well as two great halls a kitchen and stables. The most splendid remains in Adare are those of the 15th century Franciscan Friary (located in the grounds of the Adare Manor Golf Club) which can be admired from the long medieval bridge on the N20 to the north of the village.

AILLWEE CAVE *County Clare* 25 C3
A short way south of Ballyvaughan, at the edge of the limestone plateau known as the Burren, Aillwee Cave, was discovered in 1940 by a local shepherd. Well over 2 million years old, the tunnel, some 0.75 of a mile in length, is filled with stalagmites and stalactites and an illuminated underground river and waterfall.

BALLINTOBER CASTLE (or TOBERBRIDE) 22 B1
County Roscommon
Just outside the village of Ballintober of Bridget is this ruin of a huge castle dating back to about 1300. It was the principal seat of the O'Connor dynasty from the time of the Anglo-Norman invasions until the 18th century when they moved to Clonalis. Many times besieged, rarely breached, it is without a keep, but retains its twin-towered gatehouse and corner towers.

BELFAST CATHEDRAL *Belfast* 17 C2
Close to the intersection of Clifton, Donegall and York Streets and Royal Avenue, St Anne's is the Protestant Cathedral for the dioceses of Connor and Down-and-Dromore. Built in 1898, in Romanesque style, it includes mosaics by Gertrude Stein, has some very fine stained glass and is the burial place of Lord Carson, the leader of the opposition to Home Rule who died in 1935.

BELLEEK POTTERY *County Fermanagh* 14 B1
The pottery was established in the small village of Belleek in 1857 by John Caldwell Bloomfield who had inherited nearby Castle Caldwell. A keen amateur potter, he noticed that all the necessary ingredients - feldspar, water, kaolin and so on - were available locally. Within ten years, award winning highly decorated, lustrous parian ware was being made and a tour of the attractive works demonstrates its continuing production. A shop and a small museum are attached to the works.

BIRR CASTLE DEMESNE *County Offaly* 29 C1
Birr Castle has been occupied by the Parsons family since 1620 when Sir Laurence Parsons built most of the current building. Twice beseiged in the late 17th century, the Gothic facade was added in the 19th century. Although the castle is only occasionally opened to the public, the gardens are open daily and consist of a beautifully landscaped collection of trees and shrubs, the tallest box hedge in the world, and a kitchen garden, all set around a lake and waterfalls. An unusual feature is the case of the Great Telescope, built in the 1840s by the 3rd Earl of Rosse and the largest in the world until 1917. Exhibitions about the castle demesne are held in the stables.

Birr Castle

BLARNEY CASTLE & BLARNEY STONE 34 A2
County Cork
The castle is just southwest of the village of Blarney. The keep, standing on a rocky outcrop, amid 18th century parkland, was built in 1446 by Cormac MacCarthy and then lost by the MacCarthys in the 17th century, finally passing to the Colthursts who built the nearby 19th century house. The Blarney Stone lies just beneath the battlements. According to the rhyme 'A stone that whoever kisses, O he never misses to grow eloquent' but the origin of this bizarre piece of hokum is unknown, although it is said that Dermot MacCarthy was expert in using honeyed language to keep the English at bay in the 16th century.

BOYLE ABBEY *County Roscommon* 14 B3
The impressive remains of the 12th century Cistercian abbey known as Mainister na Buaille are on the north side of the market town of Boyle and are the burial place of Ireland's most famous medieval religious poet, Donnchadh Mor O'Daly, who may have been abbot here. Although badly damaged by Cromwell's army, the abbey is one of the best preserved in the country. The church is a fine example of the transition from Romanesque to Gothic and has particularly interesting carvings on the arcade capitals, whilst elsewhere the gatehouse, kitchen and cloister are all clearly in evidence.

Boyle Abbey

BUNRATTY CASTLE *nr. Limerick, County Clare* 28 A2
The original design of the roof was unknown and during the restoration was a matter of conjecture, but the remaining, magnificent keep of Bunratty Castle has been restored to how it looked at the time of its construction on the banks of the Ratty in 1460. It was probably built by the MacNamaras but was soon in the hands of the O'Briens, who became the Earls of Thomond and who occupied the castle until 1712. Widely admired in its heyday, the three storeyed keep retains its corner towers and massive arches. Inside is the vaulted entrance hall, with so-called 'sheila-na-gig' (female fertility figure) in the wall, and chapel and cellars with 16th century stucco work. Many of the rooms are filled with a fine collection of period furniture, whilst mock banquets regularly evoke the castle's colourful past. The nearby folk park has examples of traditional Irish houses and agricultural machinery and demonstrations of ancient skills.

BUNRATTY CASTLE & FOLK PARK *County Clare* 28 A2
The magnificently restored castle is described above. At its base is the folk park, a collection of buildings and artefacts that illustrate Ireland's rural life at the turn of the century. Some of the buildings were moved here from an original site elsewhere whilst others are replicas. Traditional cottages from hill and valley areas of the Shannon region are represented, as well as a blacksmiths workshop, a mill, and an entire village as it would have been at the turn of the 19th century. Demonstrations of traditional skills are regularly given.

CAHIR CASTLE *Cahir, County Tipperary* 35 C1
A pretty town, Cahir boasts this impressive castle, the largest of its type in the country, which sits on a rocky outcrop in the middle of the River Suir at the foot of the Galty Mountains. It dates back to the 15th century and was inappropriately restored in 1840. However, behinds its walls are a huge keep, a furnished great hall and two courts. Notwithstanding its solid appearance it was frequently overrun and in 1650 surrendered to Cromwell without coming to battle. There is also an exhibition on Gaelic laws and customs.

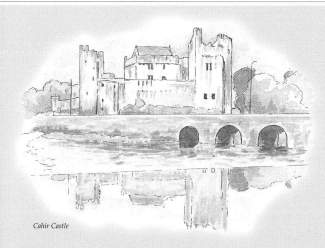

Cahir Castle

CARRICK-A-REDE ROPEBRIDGE *County Antrim* 12 B1
This curiosity, north of Ballycastle, is a 66 ft bridge of planks with wire handrails swinging 80 ft above the sea and rocks separating Larrybane Cliffs from a small rocky island. There are magnificent views out to sea to be enjoyed during the intrepid journey across the bridge. This bridge has been erected here every spring for 200 years or more for the fishermen who operate a salmon fishery on the island.

CARRICKFERGUS CASTLE 13 D3
Carrickfergus, County Antrim
Carrickfergus dates back to the end of the 12th century but is very well preserved. Among the historical events associated with it are the landing of William of Orange in 1690 and the first action by an American ship in European waters in 1778. There remain three medieval courtyards within the walls containing a massive keep, with barrel-vaulted chambers and Great Hall. It contains a goodly selection of armour and armaments.

CARROWKEEL *County Sligo* 14 B3
About 4 miles northwest of Ballinafad, just west of Lough Arrow, on the Bricklieve Mountains, is the remote site of Carrowkeel Bronze-Age passage-tomb cemetery. The setting consists of the site of an ancient village and 14 chambered cairns. It is not sure if the village, consisting of some 70 circular huts, and the burial ground, are from the same era but the cemetery, which contained cremated remains and was clearly planned, is undoubtedly one of the most important in the country.

CASTLE COOLE *County Fermanagh* 15 D2
Recently restored by the National Trust, this elegant house, the seat of the Earls of Belmore, was designed in neo-Classical style by James Wyatt and Richard Johnston at the end of the 18th century. The facade is of Portland Stone whilst the interior plaster work, of classical simplicity, was undertaken by Joseph Rose in rooms still filled with their original furniture. The lake is the home of Ireland's only breeding colony of Greylag Geese.

CASTLECALDWELL *nr. Leggs, County Fermanagh* 15 C1
The Caldwell family was responsible for the local porcelain industry, and their ruined 17th century castle is situated in a wooded peninsula on the banks of Lower Lough Erne. There are inspiring views across the lough from the gardens where wildfowl hides permit visitors to gaze undisturbed at the flocks of waterfowl that breed here, including the largest breeding colony of black scoter duck in the British Isles.

CASTLETOWN HOUSE *Celbridge, County Kildare* 27 C2
Just outside the Liffeyside village of Celbridge, Castletown, built in 1722 for the Speaker of the Irish House of Commons, William Conolly, is perhaps the largest private house in Ireland. Consisting of a central block in early Georgian or Palladian style, flanked by colonnades, Castletown was designed by the Florentine, Alessandro Galilei, and Edward Pearce, architect of the Dublin Parliament. The house has been restored through the work of the Irish Georgian Society.

CASTLE WARD 17 D3
Strangford, County Down
Situated in 600 acres of parkland, Castle Ward, now the property of the National Trust, is a half Gothic, half Palladian masterpiece built in 1765 for the 1st Viscount Bangor and his wife, each of whom favoured different styles. The family furniture is still in place, whilst the Trust has recreated aVictorian laundry. Close to the house is Old Castle Ward, a small Plantation castle built in1610.

CHRIST CHURCH CATHEDRAL *Dublin* 27 D2
The cathedral church of the Protestant archdiocese of Dublin and Glendalough, and the principal religious and ceremonial church for the former English regime, is at the heart of the medieval city. It has been the scene for many notable events, including the coronation of Lambert Simnel as Edward VI in 1487. The first cathedral was built here in 1038 and a replacement begun over a century later. Various additions were made over the following centuries but after the nave vaulting collapsed in 1562 it went through a period of neglect. Eventually the whole church was remodelled in Gothic Revival style by G.E. Street, who was also responsible for the covered footbridge linking the cathedral to the Synod Hall. The interior has some fine surviving medieval sections including the groin-vaulted crypt, and transepts, all of which date back to the 12th century, and a sprinkling of interesting monuments including the casket containing the heart of St Laurence, and the figure of Robert, 19th Earl ofKildare.

CLONONEY CASTLE *County Offaly* 23 C3
A little way to the northwest of the village of Cloghan, Clononey Castle was occupied right up to the 19th century. It consists of a well-preserved tower and 17th century bawn where there is a plaque in memory of those members of the Boleyn family exiled here after the execution of Anne Boleyn, wife of Henry VIII.

CLONALIS HOUSE *Castlerea, County Roscommon* 22 B1
In the town that was the birthplace of Oscar Wilde's father, William Wilde, the noted antiquary, Clonalis House is the 19th century version of what was once the seat of O'Conor Don, of the O'Conors of Connacht, who produced two 12th century kings of Ireland. The house is a museum devoted to the family's colourful history.

CLONMACNOISE MONASTERY *County Offaly* 23 C3
Sitting on a ridge on the banks of the Shannon, the remains of one of Ireland's first and most holy monasteries would ideally be approached by boat from Athlone. Founded in 545 by St Kiaran, a few months before his death, his tomb became an object of pilgrimage and the monastery grew to become a centre of Irish art and literature. The burial place of several Kings of Tara and Connacht, Clonmacnois has endured many fires and numerous pillagings by Irish, Viking and English.
The remains consist of two fine High Crosses, 400 memorial slabs from the 8th, 9th and 10th centuries, two Round Towers and eight churches. The 10th century West cross, with its frieze depicting St Kiaran and the local king from whom he obtained the monastery land, and the magnificently carved doorway of the Cathedral church are of particular interest.

CONG ABBEY *County Mayo* 25 C1
Although the village is best known nowadays for the impressive mock medieval castle of Ashford, now a hotel, that was built for Sir Arthur Guinness, in Irish history Cong is associated with its monastery founded in the 6th century by St Feichin. This was superseded by an Augustinian monastery in the 12th century of which the inscribed base of a cross remains in the main street, whilst the remains of the chancel of the abbey church are to be found outside the village to the southwest. It has a beautiful north door but most appealing of all are the three doorways in the remaining convent buildings, thse contain some of the finest medieval Irish carving in existence.

CRAG CAVE *County Kerry* 31 C3
Not far from Tralee, Crag Cave is really a network of limestone caves some 2.5 miles in length, discovered only in 1983. Over a million years old, they are festooned with stalactites and stalagmites, many of which have conjoined to form curtains and pillars. The Crystal Gallery is so called because of the white straw stalactites that glitter in the light.

DONEGAL CASTLE *Donegal, County Donegal* 14 B1
The late 15th century castle is just off the main square of this market town that has given its name to the county. Originally the seat of the O'Donnells, the castle tower was built by Red Hugh II O Donnell in 1505, whilst additions, including the magnificent fireplace in the banqueting hall, were made in the 17th century by a later occupant, the Planter Sir Basil Brooke, who was responsible for the fine Jacobean fortified house that forms part of the castle.

NATIONAL BOTANIC GARDENS *Dublin* 27 D2
Dublin's Botanic Gardens, in the suburb of Glasnevin, beyond the Royal Canal, were created in 1795 by the Royal Dublin Society, passing to the state in 1878. In its 50 acres there are several notable conservatories including one, over 400 ft in length, by Richard Turner who also designed for Kew in London. One of the finest

botanical gardens in Europe, it is especially noted for its conifers, cycads, herbaceous borders and orchids, and boasts a lily pond, a sunken garden and a rock garden.

Donegal Castle

DUBLIN CASTLE Dublin, *County Dublin* 27 D2

Built at the turn of the 13th century, Dublin Castle has been a gaol for many important characters throughout Irish history, as well as the seat of English power until 1922. Nonetheless, it has never had to withstand a serious assault. Its only real enemy was neglect and the whole edifice was more or less reconstructed throughout the 18th century; and although it still retains an air of fortified unity, the only substantial medievalremains are the southeast or Record tower and the layout of the Upper Castle Yard. The original moat has also been discovered.The 18th century work was the last major brick construction in Dublin and guided tours will take you through the magnificently decorated and furnished State Apartments which include St Patrick's Hall (where Irish presidents are inaugurated), the circular Supper Room in the handsome Bermingham Tower, and the Throne Room. In the Lower Castle Yard is the impressive Church of the Most Holy Trinity, or the Chapel Royal, in Gothick style.

DUBLIN CATHEDRAL *Dublin* 27 D2

St Patrick's Cathedral is the largest church in Ireland and has for much of its existence had to compete with Christchurch for its Cathedral status. Founded in 1191 and rebuilt in the 14th century it is essentially Early English in style, although damage wrought during the Cromwellian wars was only restored in the 1860s. The satirist Jonathan Swift, Dean of the Cathedral 1713-45, is buried here. The baptistry, paved with 13th century tiles, is all that remains of the first church, whilst at the west end of the nave stands the old Chapter House door. The best preserved part of the medieval church, however, is the Choir which came to be the chapel of the now defunct Order of St Patrick, instituted in 1783. Among the monuments perhaps the most impressive is the Boyle Monument, erected by the Earl of Cork in memory of his wife Catherine.

DUN AENGUS FORT 24 A2

Inishmore, Aran Islands, County Galway

Towards the far southwestern part of the island, on a spectacularly desolate slope overlooking the Atlantic, are the scattered remains of Dun Aengus (or, according to the most correct pronunciation, Doon Eeneece), one of the most important prehistoric forts in Europe, some 2500 years old. The 11 acre site consists of three enclosures with dry-stone walls up to 18 feet high. Most striking is the arrangement of jagged limestone menhirs which defend the middle wall.

DUNLUCE CASTLE (or Mermaid's Castle) 12 B1

County Antrim

Just northwest of the town of Bushmills, famous for its whiskey distillery, Dunluce Castle is dramatically situated on a high rock overlooking the sea. It was first a Macquillan stronghold, then came to the MacDonnells until the 17th century when the occupied domestic quarters fell into the sea. The earliest part dates back to the late 13th century whilst the other sections - the Scottish gatehouse, the loggia - were built at different times up to the 17th century.

DUNSOGHLY CASTLE *Finglas, County Dublin* 21 C3

Just three miles to the northwest of Finglas, Dunsoghly Castle consists of a stately residential keep-like tower on three floors buttressed by rectangular corner turrets. It was built in the 15th century by Thomas Plunkett, Chief Justice of the King's Bench, whilst the nearby chapel was built in 1573 by Sir John Plunkett, also Chief Justice but for the Queen's Bench.

FOTA HOUSE Carrigtwohill, *County Cork* 34 B2

Fota House is on Fota Island which, accessible by causeways, sits in the River Lee Estuary. Built in 1820 for the Earls of Barrymore, it is a handsome Regency house with a fine collection of 18th and 19th century furniture and Irish landscape paintings. In the surrounding grounds is the internationally renowned arboretum begun in the 1820s with its collections of rare shrubs and semi-tropical and coniferous trees, which has so far escaped a threatened tourist development. There is also a wildlife park and bee garden.

GALLARUS ORATORY

nr. Ballyferriter, County Kerry 30 A3

On the beautiful Dingle peninsula, at Lateevmore, which is about 2 miles east of Ballyferriter, is Gallarus oratory, a corbel-roofed dry-stone structure of remarkable perfection and completely waterproof. A Christian chapel that is over one thousand years old, it lacks only the crosses that once decorated the roof.

GIANTS CAUSEWAY *County Antrim* 12 B1

This monumental terrace of steps some 300ft high stretches out into the ocean on the north Antrim coast between Port Ganny and Port Noffer. It resulted from gigantic outpourings of volcanic basalt some 60 million years ago. The rock cooled into two distinct formations. Firstly, a lower layer of thousands of regular hexagonal colums and secondly , an upper layer of slim uneven prisms. This amazing piece of coastline now belongs to The National Trust, who have created a coastal path from the Causeway to Dunseverick. The Visitor Centre has an exhibition and audiovisual theatre, which outline the geological history of the Causeway.

Giant's Causeway

GLIN CASTLE *County Limerick* 31 D2

The village of Glin lies on the south shore of the Shannon Estuary. The Fitzgeralds, Knight of Glin, have lived here for over 700 years, first in a castle in the village itself, of which a fragment still remains; and then in Glin Castle, a Georgian-Gothick construction to the west of the village which dates from 1770 and which is still occupied by the family. Set in charming gardens, the house is decorated with fine plasterwork and hung with an interesting painting collection.

GRIANAN OF AILEACH *County Donegal* 11 D2

Five miles northeast of Newtowncunningham, on Greenan Mountain, this fort consists of a huge cashel (stone fort), probably dating from the early Christian period, standing at the centre of a series of three earthen banks covering 4 acres, which are either late Bronze or early Iron Age. An important stronghold of the Christian kingdom of Aileach, it retained a mythological importance long after its strategic value had passed away. There are, however, still wonderful views across the Foyle and Swilly.

HOWTH CASTLE GARDENS *Howth, County Dublin* 27 D2

Ten miles to the northeast of Dublin, Howth is a fishing port and resort. Howth Castle has been the seat of the Lawrence family since the 16th century although the family had settled in the area some 400 years previously. The castle (private) dates from 1564 and the beautiful gardens, for which soil had to be brought by the sackful by the castle staff in 1850, are renowned for their azaleas, and 2000 varieties of rhododendrons.

JAPANESE GARDENS *Tully, County Kildare* 26 B2

In the grounds of the National Stud at Tully, a short distance east of Kildare Town, the Japanese Gardens were planted by the Japanese gardener, Eida, and his son Minoru, between 1906 and 1910. Symbolising the ages of man from birth to death, the route takes you from the Gate of Oblivion and the Cave of Birth to the Garden of Eternity via the Hill of Ambition and the Well of Ambition. The Zen Meditation Garden was added in 1976.

KELLS PRIORY *County Kilkenny*   29 D3
In 1193 a priory was founded in Kells for Canons Regular of St Augustine from Bodmin in Cornwall. The impressive remains, 5 acres surrounded by substantial medieval fortified walls, with mostly complete 15th century dwelling towers, are divided into two courts by a branch of the river, in the northernmost of which are the remains of the church, with traces of medieval paving tiles, and the ruined claustral buildings.

Howth Castle Gardens

KING JOHN'S CASTLE *Carlingford, County Louth*   21 C1
The small seaport of Carlingford, on the unspoilt Cooley Peninsula, is located at the foot of the 1935 foot Slieve Foye, overlooking Carlingford Lough. The castle remains, strategically located to command the quay, dating back to the late 12th century, played host to King John who stayed here on his way to attack Hugh de Lacy, at Carrickfergus. It has an unusual D-shape while the west gateway was designed to allow the entry of only one horseman at a time. The remains of an earlier castle include the southwest tower and the west wall.

KING JOHN'S CASTLE *Limerick, County Limerick*   28 A2
In the Old Town of Limerick (on a sort of island formed by the River Shannon and the River Abbey), the 13th century castle, the most formidable English stronghold in western Ireland, is a fine example of Norman fortified architecture. It has recently been partly converted into a museum which displays antique armaments (catapults and battering rams) and tells of the castle's role in Limerick's dramatic history.

KNOWTH TOMB (BRÚ NA BÓINNE) *County Meath*   20 B2
Almost 2 miles to the northwest of the best known cairn at Newgrange, Knowth is another of the passage-tombs at the Bend of the Boyne. Built some 3000 years BC it is up to 50 ft high and 280 ft in diameter. Surrounded by a number of other, smaller cairns, the main cairn contains 2 tombs, the most westerly of which is 100 feet in length and different from the others in that it is lintelled and straighter; whilst the other is cruciform, with a corbelled roof. A quite considerable amount of ornamentation was discovered along with the cremated remains. It continued to be used up to the Iron Age when it seems also to have become a fortress. There is no direct access to Knowth or Newgrange Tombs. Visitors should use the minibus service that runs from Brú na Bóinne Visitor Centre.

LISMORE CASTLE GARDENS   35 C1
Lismore, County Waterford
The castle, handsomely located above the Blackwater, was built in the 19th century by Joseph Paxton, architect of the Crystal Palace in London, for the 6th Duke of Devonshire, incorporating the remains of the medieval castle erected by Prince John of England in 1185. The castle (private) is partially surrounded by delightful walled gardens, with areas of woodland, shrubberies, and a Yew Walk. In spring the gardens are at their best when the camellias and magnolias are in flower. The Elizabethan poet Edmund Spenser is said to have composed part of the Faerie Queene in the grounds.

LISSADELL HOUSE *Raghly, County Sligo*   14 A2
Just over four miles outside the hamlet of Raghly which hangs off a promontory on the north side of Sligo Bay, Lissadell House, situated in conifer clad parkland overlooking the sea, was built in 19th century Classical style for the patriotic Gore-Booth family. The Arctic explorer Sir Henry Gore-Booth was born here, as were his daughters Eva, the poetess, and Constance, who became the first woman member of the British House of Commons, but who chose to sit instead in the revolutionary Dail Eireann as minister for Labour. Refreshments are still served in the old-fashioned kitchen.

MARBLE ARCH CAVES *County Fermanagh*   15 C2
This system of caves, about 10 miles southwest of Enniskillen, has been formed by the action of 3 streams on a bed of Dartry limestone on 2,188 ft Mount Cuilcagh. Underground they converge to form a single river, the Cladagh, which flows via the 30ft limestone Marble Arch into Lough Macnean. The tour of the cave includes a boat ride on the underground lake and the presentation of an array of imaginatively illuminated and named rock formations, one of which, a stalactite, is over 7 feet long.

MELLIFONT ABBEY *County Louth*   20 B2
Four miles northwest of Drogheda, Mellifont was Ireland's first Cistercian abbey. Founded in 1140 by the King of Uriel, at the instigation of St Malachy, who had been inspired by St Bernard's work at Clairvaux, the abbey became the home of the Moore family after its suppression in 1539. Though scattered, the remains are of great interest and include portions of the Romanesque cloister arcade, the 13th century chapter house extension, and the octagonal washroom.

MONEA CASTLE *County Fermanagh*   15 C2
About 6 miles northwest of Enniskillen, Monea Castle was built in 1618 by the Rev. Malcolm Hamilton in Scottish Plantation style. It was burnt out in the 18th century but is in a reasonable state of preservation and its remaining two circular towers at the front and its crow-stepped gables add to its Scottish flavour.

MOUNT STEWART HOUSE
nr. Newtownards, County Down   17 D2
The 18th century former seat of the Marquess of Londonderry, and childhood home of Lord Castlereagh, the 19th century British Prime Minister, now belongs to the National Trust. A severely Classical building, it sits amid 80 acres of gardens renowned for their many rare plants, trees and fanciful topiary. The Temple of the Winds, also in the grounds, is an exquisite banqueting hall built in 1785.

MOUNT USHER GARDENS *Ashford, County Wicklow*   27 D3
Next to the village of Ashford, charmingly located by the River Vartry, the gardens of Mount Usher are made up of 20 acres planted with over 5000 species of flora. Including many subtropical plants, the naturalised gardens, laid out in 1868 by Edward Walpole, of a Dublin family of linen manufacturers, are famous for the Eucalyptus and Eucryphia collections and offer some fine woodland walks.

MURLOUGH *Newcastle, County Down*   17 D3
About two miles to the north of Newcastle is this area of sand dunes, some of which were formed over 5000 years ago, stretching from the Carrigs River and the shore of Dundrum Bay. A wild haven for all types of sea and water birds, it is also a place where wild flowers grow in profusion.

NAVAN FORT *County Armagh*   16 B3
A little way to the west of the town of Armagh, the remains at Navan are of an 18 acre hill fort, crowned by a ceremonial tumulus, which together form the last remains of the seat of Ulster kings between 350 BC and 332 AD. It is also the Emhain Macha, the legendary home of Cu Chulainn, one of the knights of Ulster mythology.

NESS WOOD COUNTRY PARK *County Londonderry*   12 A2
The 46 acres of woodland were originally dominated by oak trees but many other species were added from the 17th century. The highlight of Ness, however, is the spectacular 30 ft waterfall, part of the River Burntollet, which since the last Ice Age has also created a series of gorges and rapids through the metamorphic rock.

PARKE'S CASTLE *County Leitrim*   14 B2
On the banks of Lough Gill, in Kilmore, close to Dromahaire, Parkes Castle is a Plantation castle in markedly Scottish style built in the 17th century on the site of an earlier castle. In a good state of preservation, its courtyard walls are fortified with picturesque towers and gatehouses and it played a key role in the war of 1641 - 52. There is a permanent exhibition about the area as well as an excellent audio visual show.

POWERSCOURT GARDEN   27 D2
nr. Enniskerry, County Wicklow
A disastrous fire in the 1970's has left only the shell of Powerscourt House, built in 1730 for Viscount Powerscourt by the Huguenot architect Richard Cassels and then enlarged and altered in the 19th century. Its mountain setting is magnificent, however, as are the gardens with their handsome 19th century terraces, Monkey Puzzle Avenue, and Japanese Garden, added

in 1908. In the grounds, and approachable by a separate car entrance, is a spectacular 400 feet waterfall.

PROLEEK DOLMEN *County Louth* **21 C1**
To the north of Dundalk, the capital of Louth, in Aghnaskeagh, are two prehistoric cairns and a fort. Nearby Proleek is the site of the so called 'Giant's Load', a tomb that is the legendary grave of Para Bui Mor Mhac Seoidin, the Scottish giant who challenged Finn MacCool. A trio of smaller upright stones supporting a larger capstone, the tomb dates back 3000 BC. It is thought that the capstone was hauled into position by means of a vanished earthen ramp.

Proleek Dolmen

QUIN ABBEY *County Clare* **28 A2**
The village of Quin is noted for a Franciscan friary founded in the early 15th century, the first Observantine house in Ireland. The ruins, incorporating an earlier castle, are sufficiently well preserved to clearly demonstrate the layout of a medieval friary.

RING OF KERRY *County Kerry* **36 B1**
The Ring of Kerry is a famous circular scenic route of about 115 miles around the Iveragh Peninsula. Clearly it can begin at any point on the route but the town of Killarney is generally considered the gateway to the peninsula, even if the best section lies between Kenmare and Killorglin. The fine mountain and maritime scenery is a constant companion but the route passes through or near to a number of interesting places including Sneem, with its old Anglican church; the 2000 year fort at Staigue; Derrynane National Historic Park, the former home of Daniel O'Connell; the resort of Waterville; Coomakesta Pass; Valencia Island; Knocknadobar Mountain; Cahergall Fort; Leacanabuaile Fort; Rossbeigh Strand; Glenbeigh with its Bog Village Museum; and Lough Caragh and its views across to Macgillycuddy's Reeks. Whilst the principal route more or less follows the coast, some of the finest scenery is to be found along the unmarked roads running through the interior of the peninsula.

ROCK OF CASHEL *County Tipperary* **29 C3**
One of the most spectacular sights in Ireland, the Rock of Cashel is a steep limestone outcrop surmounted by the ruins of the ancient capital of the Kings of Munster. According to legend, St Patrick baptised Corc the Third here; and Brian Boru, High King of Ireland, was crowned here in 977. In 1101 King Murtagh O'Brien donated the rock to the church after which it became the See of the Archbishopric of Munster. The ruins are extensive and fascinating. Cormac's Chapel, built in the 1130s in a style sometimes called Hiberno-Romanesque, contains a magnificent carved 11th century sarcophagus; whilst the carved Cross of St Patrick is set into the coronation stone of the Kings of Munster. The main cathedral is essentially 13th century and although it has suffered pillage and neglect, it remains a fine example of Irish Gothic. There are remarkable views across the surrounding countryside from the part of the cathedral known as the Castle, built to house the 15th century bishops.

ROCK OF DUNAMASE *County Laois* **26 B3**
Close to Portlaoise, on the Stradbally road, a large ruined castle sits on top of this 150 ft rock, all that remains of what was a considerable fortress, destroyed in the Cromwellian wars. Through the marriage of the daughter of the King of Leinster, it had moved into Anglo Norman hands in the late 12th century, and was twice rebuilt, in 1250 and at the end of the 15th century. There are fine views to be had from the summit of the rock

where the remains of the gatehouse, walls and 13th century keep are still in evidence.

RUSSBOROUGH HOUSE
Blessington, County Wicklow **27 C2**
One of Ireland's foremost Palladian houses was built for a Dublin brewer, Joseph Leeson, 1st Earl of Milltown, by Richard Cassels and Francis Bindon in the 1740s. A granite exterior conceals an interior coated in extravagant stucco work and bearing a fine painting collection.

ST. CANICE CATHEDRAL *Kilkenny City* **32 A1**
The city actually takes its name from St Canice who founded a monastery here in the 6th century, upon the site of which stands the current cathedral. Much restored in the 19th century, it is the second largest medieval cathedral in Ireland. Inside is the finest display of burial monuments in the country whilst the high round tower adjacent to the cathedral is the only substantial relic from the monastery. The building is essentially 13th century and the oldest tomb is also from this period, although the oldest decipherable slab is that of Jose Kyteler, the father of Alice Kyteler, tried for witchcraft in 1323.

SCRABO *Newtownards, County Down* **17 D2**
The landscape roundabout is dominated by Scrabo Hill, a layer of volcanic rock over a mound of sandstone dominates the landscape. It is crowned by Scrabo Tower, erected in 1857 in memory of the third Marquess of Londonderry. Built in saturnine dolerite, and sandstone, it now houses a museum about the surrounding countryside, some of which is made up of 19th century beech and mixed woodland. There are magnificent views across Strangford Lough.

STAIGUE STONE FORT *nr. Castlecove, County Kerry* **36 B2**
Amid the beautiful scenery overlooking Kenmare Bay, Staigue is a stone 2500 year old ringfort made up of a 13 ft thick rampart divided into terraces and linked by a system of stairways.

THOOR BALLYLEE *County Galway* **28 A1**
The 16th century tower of Ballylee Castle, the Thoor Ballylee of Yeat's poems, is 5 miles northeast of the market town of Gort. A charming ivy clad tower on the banks of the river, Ballylee was Yeat's home in the 1920s, where he wrote the volume of poems entitled The Tower. After he left in 1929 the tower became a ruin once more until its restoration as a Yeats Museum in 1965.

Quin Abbey

WESTPORT HOUSE *County Mayo* **18 B3**
Adjacent to the pretty village of Westport, planned by James Wyatt for the Marquess of Sligo, the house, built in about 1730, is by Richard Cassels, with additions by Wyatt in 1778. The house, entered from the Quay, contains a mixture of antique silver and furniture and modern entertainment facilities, whilst in the demesne itself is an ornamental lake, created by controlling the tides of Clew Bay, and a miniature zoo.

KEY TO MAP SYMBOLS

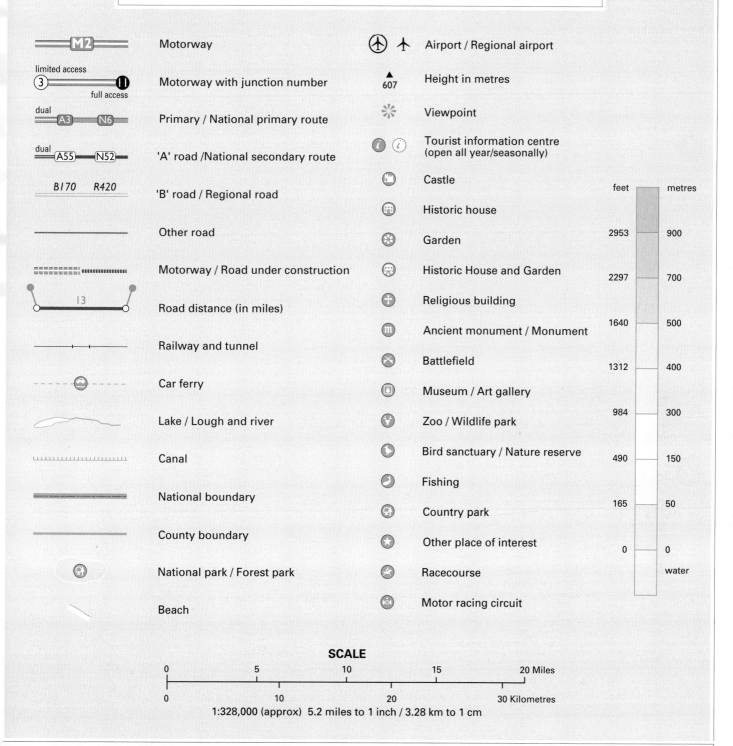

	Motorway		Airport / Regional airport
limited access / full access	Motorway with junction number	607	Height in metres
dual A3 N6	Primary / National primary route		Viewpoint
dual A55 N52	'A' road /National secondary route		Tourist information centre (open all year/seasonally)
B170 R420	'B' road / Regional road		Castle
	Other road		Historic house
	Motorway / Road under construction		Garden
13	Road distance (in miles)		Historic House and Garden
	Railway and tunnel		Religious building
	Car ferry		Ancient monument / Monument
	Lake / Lough and river		Battlefield
	Canal		Museum / Art gallery
	National boundary		Zoo / Wildlife park
	County boundary		Bird sanctuary / Nature reserve
	National park / Forest park		Fishing
	Beach		Country park
			Other place of interest
			Racecourse
			Motor racing circuit

feet	metres
2953	900
2297	700
1640	500
1312	400
984	300
490	150
165	50
0	0
	water

SCALE

0 5 10 15 20 Miles
0 10 20 30 Kilometres
1:328,000 (approx) 5.2 miles to 1 inch / 3.28 km to 1 cm

ADDITIONAL INFORMATION ON CITY & TOWN PLANS

	Main road / Throughroute	P	Car park
	Pedestrian street	WC	Public toilets
	Shopping street	Pol •	Police station
	Place of interest	✝ +	Cathedral / Church
	Railway station	→	One way street

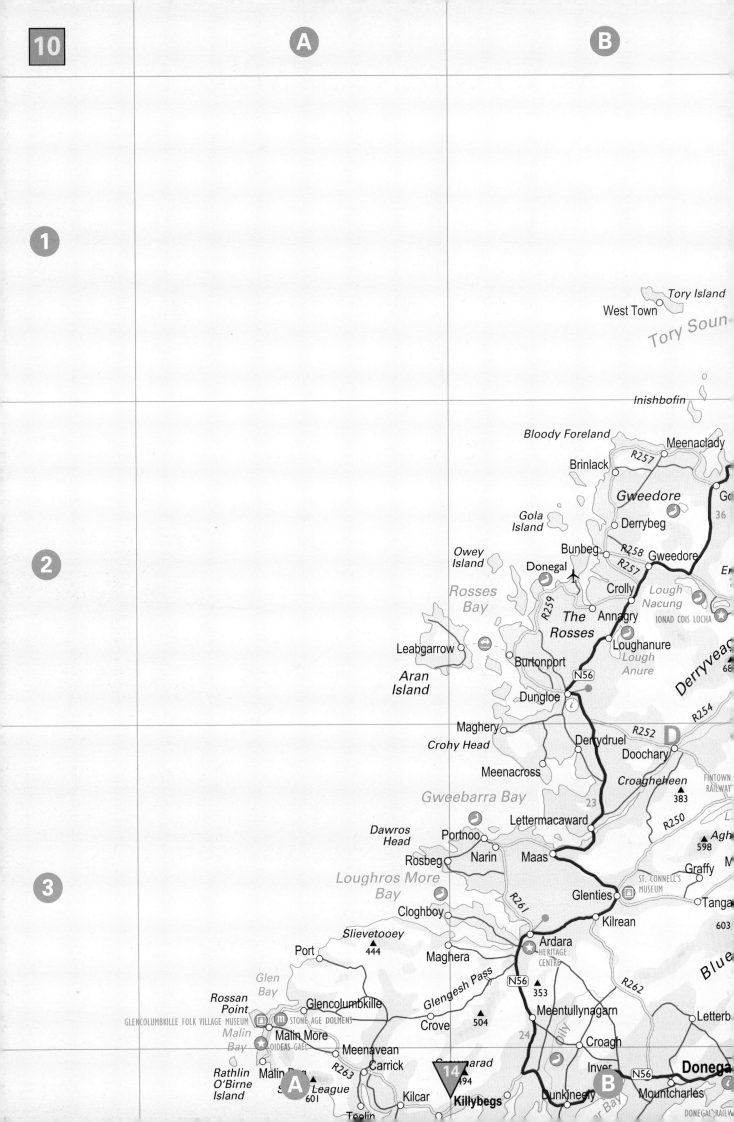

A

B

1

Tory Island

West Town

Tory Soun

Inishbofin

Bloody Foreland

Meenaclady

R257

Brinlack

Gweedore

Gola
Island

Derrybeg

Bunbeg

R258

Gweedore

Donegal

R257

Owey
Island

Crolly

2

R259

The
Rosses

Annagry

Lough
Nacung

Rosses
Bay

IONAD COIS LOCHA

Leabgarrow

Burtonport

Loughanure

Lough
Anure

Derryvea

68

Aran
Island

N56

R254

Dungloe

Maghery

Derrydruel

R252

Doochary

D

Crohy Head

Meenacross

Croagheheen

383

FINTOWN
RAILWAY

Gweebarra Bay

Lettermacaward

23

R250

Dawros
Head

Portnoo

Agh

598

Rosbeg

Narin

Maas

Graffy

3

Loughros More
Bay

R261

Glenties

ST. CONNELL'S
MUSEUM

Tanga

Cloghboy

Kilrean

603

Slievetooey

Ardara

HERITAGE
CENTRE

Port

444

Maghera

Blue

Glen
Bay

Glengesh Pass

N56

353

R262

Letterb

Rossan
Point

Glencolumbkille

Crove

504

Meentullynagarn

GLENCOLUMBKILLE FOLK VILLAGE MUSEUM

STONE AGE DOLMENS

24

Croagh

Malin
Bay

Malin More

OIDEAS GAEL

Meenavean

Carrick

R263

Inver

N56

Donega

Rathlin
O'Birne
Island

Malin B

A

League

601

Kilcar

14

arad

494

Dunkineely

B

Mountcharles

Toolin

Killybegs

DONEGAL RAILW

Ardnacross
Bay

Benn
Hea

Machrihanish Bay

1

RE RESERVE

BOATHOUSE
CENTRE

*Rathlin
Island*

Mull of Kintyre

N
o
r
t
h

nduff
BONAMARGY
FRIARY
Fair Head
Ballyvoy
Torr Head
Torr

Ballycastle

DUNLOUGHAN
FARM-MUSEUM

317
ocklayd

A2

WATERTOP
OPEN FARM
17

Runabay Head

Cushendun

Knocknacarry

Glendun

noe
e

Cushendall

Trostan
554
B14
Glenariff
10

Garron Point

C
h
a
n
n
e
l

To Troon 4 hrs

2

To Cairnryan 1 - 2 1/4 hrs

A43

A2

*Carnlough
Bay*

To Troon 2 1/2 hrs

To Stranraer 1 3/4 - 3 1/4 hrs

rkey
s
lls

Antrim Hills

**Glenariff
Forest Park**
18

Newtown
Crommelin

Carnlough
Glenarm

*The Maidens or
Hulin Rocks*

B64

Martinstown
A42
B97

MacGregor's Corner
The Sheddings
15

A43
15
Buckna
Glenarm
Feystown
A2

Ballygalley Head
Ballygalley
CARNFUNNOCK

Drains Bay

3

NTRI M

Broughshane
A42

Slemish
437

B94

Agnew's Hill
476

B148

Larne

To Fleetwood 8 hrs

1
ORROW'S SHOP
MUSEUM
2
10

A36

Moorfields
20

Kilwaughter

Portmuck
Island Magee

A26
B98
B53
Shoptown

A36
B100

Glynn

*Larne
Lough*

B90

Kells
Connor
Tildarg

B99

Glenoe

B150

Chapeltown
B59
B94
11

Ballycarry

LOUGHSIDE OPEN
DAIRY FARM
A2

Black Head

10

ANTRIM CASTLE
GARDENS

Ballynure

KNIGHT RIDE
& HERITAGE PLAZA

B149

B90

Whitehead

122

PATTERSON'S
SPADE MILL (NT)
B95
Ballyclare

Milebush

*See Town Plan on Page 40
for Belfast Places Of Interest*

A6

M2
A57
Doagh

A8

B58
19
Eden

*Mew
Island*

To Heysham 4 hrs (summer only)

6
B95
ROUND TOWER

4
B56
B59
B90
A2

ANDREW JACKSON CENTRE
Carrickfergus
CARRICKFERGUS CASTLE

PICKIE FAMILY
FUN PARK

Groomsport
A2

To Douglas 2 3/4 hrs

Antrim
Templepatrick
A6

Greenisland
Grey Pt
CRAWFORDSBURN

**Helen's
Bay**

Crawfordsburn

*Copeland
Island*

To Liverpool 7 1/2 hrs

Belfast
International
A57
B39

Newtownabbey
CAVE-HILL
HERITAGE CENTRE
ZOO

Craigavad

*Belfast
Lough*

Bangor
A48
B21

Donaghadee
NORTH DOWN
HERITAGE CENTRE
To ... (summer only)

ve
A.C.T
GARDEN
Nutt's
Cr

CAVE
HILL
CITY HALL

Whitehouse
17

A6
B **Belfast
City**

Holywood

ULSTER FOLK
& TRANSPORT MUSEUM

Conlig

Craigantlet

SOMME
HER. CEN.
A21

Six Road Ends
B172

Millisle

Crumlin
A52
B101
Dundrod

B154

BELFAST

A26

Dundonald

BALLYCOPELAND WINDMILL

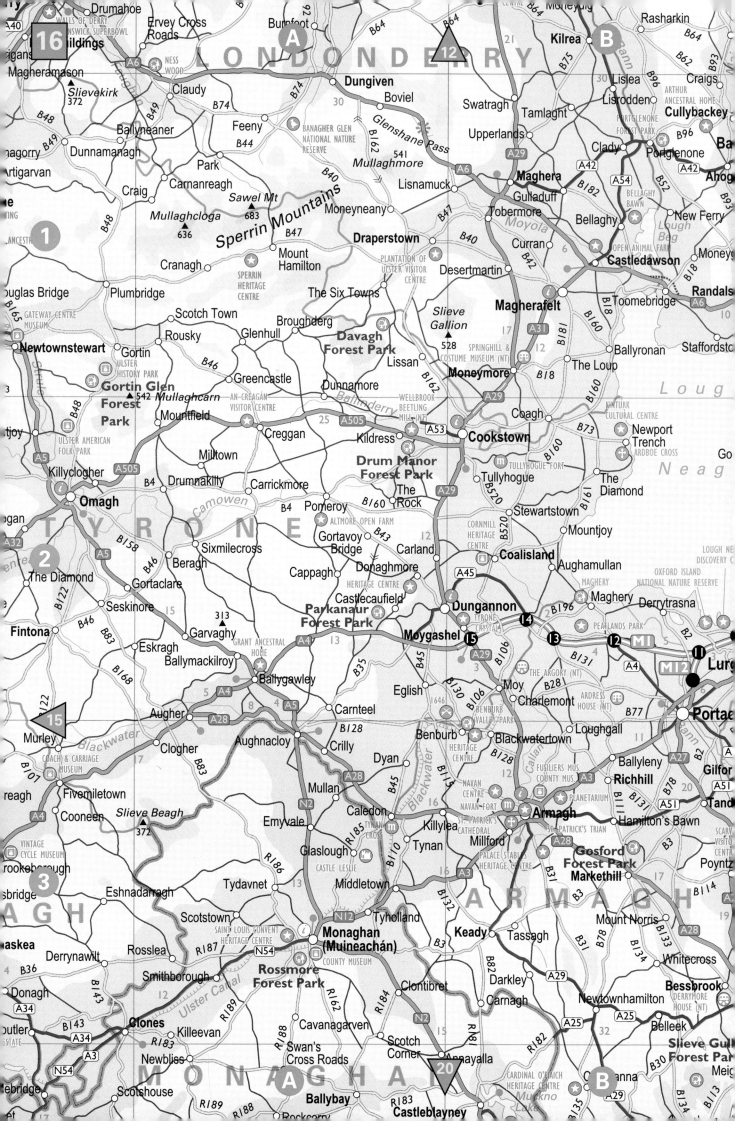

A   B

1

2

3

Erris Head
Aghadoon
DOONAMO FORT
Corclogh
Belmullet
Binghamstown
The Mullet
R313
R313
Trawmore Bay
Inishkea North
Inishkea South
Aghleam
Fallmore
Duvillaun More
Blacksod
Bay
Doohooma
Gweensalia
Stonefield
Knocknalina
Barnatra
R314
Bunnahowen
R313
Attavalley

Stags of
Broad Haven
Benwee Head
Portacloy
Porturlin
Belderg
Broad
Haven
Pollatomish
Bunalty
Glenamoy
Carrowmore
Lake
Bangor Erris
Owenmore
N59

CEIDE FIELDS &
VISITOR CENTRE
Maumake
380
Bal
C
Sheskin
Doobehy
Lough
Dahybaun
26
Bellacorick
Moyla
R312 Deel
Slieve Car
772
Keenagh
R3
Nephin Beg
629
Derreen
Birreencorragh
700

Slieve More
672
Croaghaun
668
Achill Head
Dooagh   Keel
R319
Bunacurry
Valley
Doogort
Annagh
Island
Achill
Achill
Island
Dooega
Corraun
Peninsula
Cloughmore
Corraun
Achillbeg
Island
Clare
Island
Ballytoohy

Srahnamanragh
Bridge
Doona
Ballycroy
Owenduff
Claggan
39
Mulrany
Rosturk
Dooghbeg

Nephin Beg Range
Cushcamcarragh
714
Lough
Feeagh
Furnace
Lough
Newport
Srahmore
M   A
R317
N59
Clogher
R311
(Caislea
Cas
Kilmeena

Caher
Island
Inishturk

Clew Bay
NATIONAL FAMINE MONUMENT
& CROAGH PATRICK
INFORMATION CENTRE
Roonah
Quay
Louisburgh
GRANUAILE
VISITORS CENTRE
M u r r i s k
Mullagh
SRAHMEE
MEGALITHIC TOMB
Killadoon
Cregganbaun
Kinnadoohy
R335
Murrisk
R335
765 Croagh Patrick
Liscarney
Cuilmore
Westport Quay
Westport
CLEW BAY
HERITAGE CENTRE
WESTPORT
HOUSE
Islandea
Loug
N5
11
Aghago
Cordarragh
Carrowkennedy

Inishbofin
Inishshark
Cashleen
Rinvyle
Ballynakill
Bay
Tully Cross
Killary
Harbour
Salruck
Benbury ▲795
Mwe
24
Glennagevlagh
Bengorm
702
Aasleagh
650
Devil's
try Mts
41
Tourma
Benwee
682
N59

B80
Forest Park **Newcastle**
Hilltown

C **D** **1**

B8 A25
Mayobridge Slieve Donard 85 ▲ △ **17**
A2

Mourne Mountains SILENT VALLEY RESERVOIRS

MUSEUM & ARTS CENTRE **Silent Valley Reservoir**

B7 BURREN HERITAGE CENTRE

A2 Burren **Kilbroney Forest Park** Attica B27 CORN MILL Mullartown

Warrenpoint ROSTREVOR OAKWOOD **Annalong**

eath **Rostrevor** Ballymartin

Carlingford Lough R173 25

avensdale 588 ▲ GREENCASTLE **Kilkeel**

Carlingford Greenore Greencastle

HOLY TRINITY HERITAGE CENTRE KING JOHN'S CASTLE Cranfield Point

Grange *Bullagon Point*

R173 Rathcor

ock

Dundalk

Bay

ingham

Dunany Point

nnagassan

Togher Port

R166

Grangebellow

Clogher Head

Clogherhead

enny

Termonfeckin

R167 Baltray

rogheda (Droichead Átha)

R150 **Bettystown**

MILLMOUNT MUS. Laytown

Julianstown SONAIRTE NATIONAL ECOLOGY CENTRE

ewstown N1 Gormanstown

R108 Stamullen **Balbriggan**

FOUR KNOCKS MEGALITHIC TOMB **Skerries**

Naul Balrothery ARDGILLAN CASTLE

R122 Damastown R127

R128 LUSK HERITAGE CENTRE **Rush**

Ballyboghil 25 **Lusk**

bourne R129 R126 NEWBRIDGE HOUSE & FARM

hmore R108 R125 **Portrane** *Lambay Island*

Donabate

Swords N1

R107

Dublin

M1 **Malahide**

TALBOT BOTANIC GARDENS, MALAHIDE CASTLE & FRY MODEL RAILWAY

4 3 **Portmarnock**

5 *Ireland's Eye*

Coolock Howth

BOTANIC GARDENS R105 HOWTH CASTLE GARDENS NATIONAL TRANSPORT

THE CASINO

Drumcondra **C** *Dublin Bay* **27**

ZOO erston **DUBLIN (Baile Átha Cliath)**

NAGH

I R I S H

S E A

To Douglas 2 3/4 hrs (summer only)

To Liverpool 3 3/4 - 9 1/2 hrs

To Mostyn Quay 6 hrs

See Town Plan on Page 42 for Dublin Places Of Interest

D

2

3

To Holyhead 1 3/4 - 3 1/4 hrs

Inishbofin

Inishark

A

Kinnadooh

Cuilmore

Carrowkennedy

B

N59

Benbury ▲795

△ 18

R335

Tourma

▲ 819
Mweelrea

Bengorm

41

Cashleen   Rinvyle   Salruck

Killary Harbour

Aasleagh

Partry Mts

650   Benwee
682

Ballynakill Bay

702

Glennagevlagh

Tully Cross

Lough Fee

Aughrus More

OCEANS ALIVE

KYLEMORE ABBEY

Letterfrack

Leenane
Mother

Devil's

Finny

Leenane Cultural Centre

Maumturk Mts

R336

Joyce's Country

Cleggan

N59

Benwee

Moyard

Connemara National Park

R334

R345

Omey Island

1

Benbaun
730

Benbaun

667

Maam

Curraun

Clifden

DAN O' HARA'S HOMESTEAD

The Twelve Pins

Bencorr
712

Lough Inagh

Co

613

Derrylea

Mannin Bay

Ballinaboy

C o n n e m a r a

Recess

R336

Derryneen

Maam Cross

Doonloughan

Ballynahinch

R342

R340

N59

49

Ballyconneely

Toombeola

Derryerglinn

R341

Cashel

Ballyconneely Bay

Roundstone

CASHEL HOUSE HOTEL & GARDEN

TEACH AN PHIARSAIGH
(PEARSE'S COTTAGE)

Gortmore

Screeb

Bertraghboy Bay

Derryrush

Glinsk

R340

Rosmuck

Kinvarra

I a r

Moyrus

Garrivinnagh

Carna

Kilkieran

Glencmurrin Lough

Ard

Ardmore

R374

Costelloe

Mweenish Island

Lettercallow

R343

Rossaveel

2

Carraroe

Lettermullen

Gorumna Island

Golam Head

Connemara ✈ Inveran

North Sound

G a l w a

Onaght

Inishmore

DUN AENGUS FORT

Kilronan

ARAN ISLANDS HERITAGE CENTRE
(IONAD ARAINN)

Inishmaan

Killeany

Inisheer

Aran Islands

South Sound

Doolin

Doolin Point

3

Cliffs of Moher

R478

CLIFFS OF
& O'BRIEN

Kilconnel

Hag's Head   Liscannor

Lah

Liscannor Bay

Rinneen

A

B

Spanish Point

Mil
Ma

Mal Bay

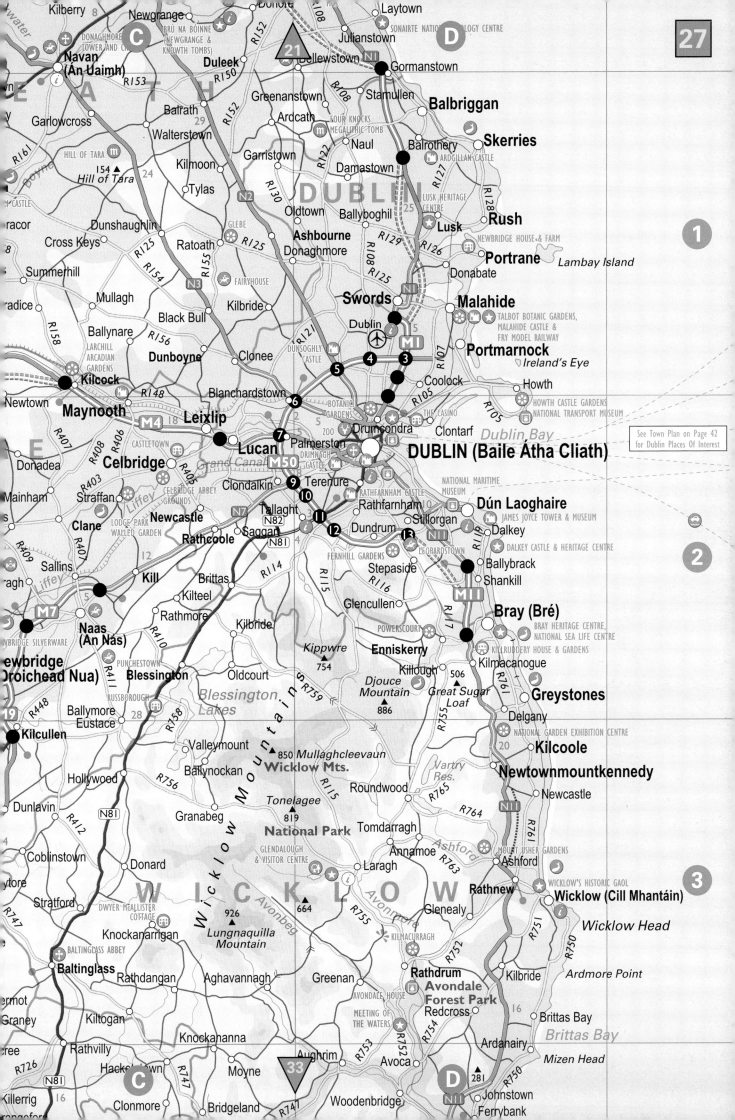

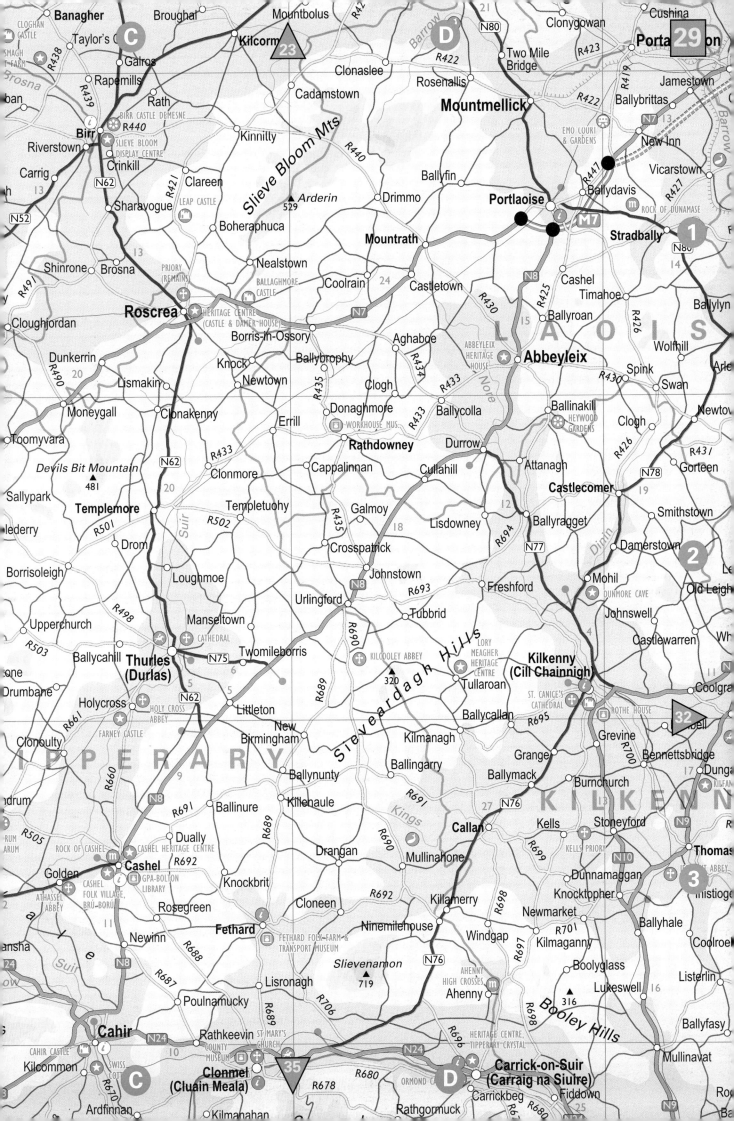

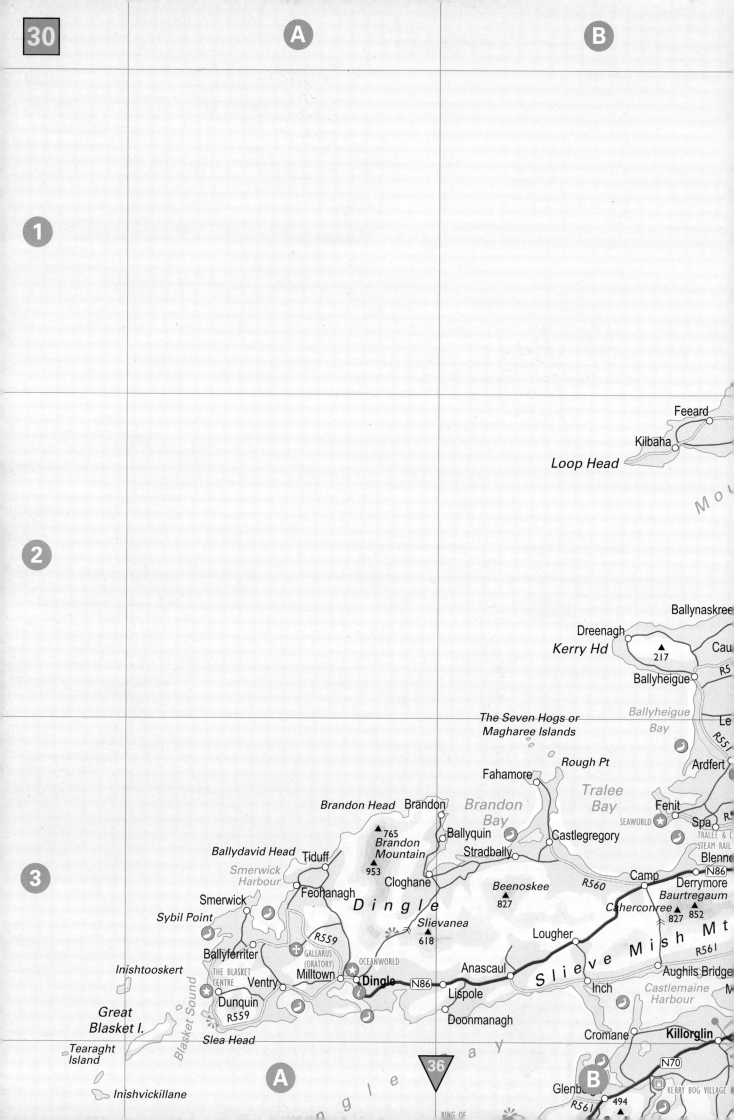

A

B

1

2

Feeard

Kilbaha

Loop Head

Mou

Ballynaskree

Dreenagh

Kerry Hd   ▲ 217   Cau

R5

Ballyheigue

Ballyheigue Bay   Le

R551

The Seven Hogs or
Magharee Islands

Ardfert

Rough Pt

Fahamore

Tralee Bay

Fenit

SEAWORLD ⭐   Spa   R*

Brandon Head   Brandon

Brandon Bay

Ballyquin

TRALEE &
STEAM RAIL

3

Ballydavid Head   Tiduff

▲ 765
Brandon
Mountain

Stradbally

Castlegregory

Blenne

N86

Smerwick Harbour

▲ 953

Cloghane

R560   Camp

Derrymore

Feohanagh

Beenoskee
▲ 827

Baurtregaum

Smerwick

Dingle

Caherconree ▲   ▲ 852
827

Sybil Point

Slievanea
▲ 618

Lougher

R559

Slieve Mish Mt

Ballyferriter

R561

✛ GALLARUS
(ORATORY)

OCEANWORLD

Anascaul

Aughils Bridge

Inishtooskert

THE BLASKET
CENTRE   Ventry

Milltown

ℹ **Dingle**   N86

Inch

*Castlemaine
Harbour*

⭐ Dunquin

R559

Lispole

Doonmanagh

*Great
Blasket I.*

Cromane

Killorglin

*Tearaght
Island*

Slea Head

KERRY BOG VILLAGE

N70

A

▽ 36

B

Glenbe

Inishvickillane

R561   494

RING OF

TRAVELLING IN IRELAND

MOTORING

EU nationals require a driving licence from their own country; other nationals require an international driving licence. The car should be accompanied by its registration papers and should either carry an approved nationality plate or EU licence plates. Full insurance is necessary and the green card, though no longer compulsory, is convenient proof of cover.

As for the highway code, traffic drives on the left. Priority should be given to traffic on roundabouts and on main roads.

If fitted, a seat belt must be worn. Children under 3 years of age (4 in Republic of Ireland) must wear an appropriate child restraint. Children aged 3-11 (up to 150 cms in height) must wear an appropriate child restraint or, if unavailable, an adult seat belt. If adult seat belts are not installed in the rear, children may legally travel unrestrained. Rear facing child restraints should not be used where there is a frontal air bag.

Parking offences in the Republic are sometimes subject to on-the-spot fines. In Northern Ireland cars must not be left unattended in control zones of town centres, although this regulation is subject to change at any time.

Unless signs instruct otherwise, a general speed limit of 60mph applies on all roads except for motorways (70mph), in built up areas (30mph) and, in Northern Ireland, on dual carriageways (70mph). Roads in the North are graded as in the rest of the United Kingdom whilst in the Republic there are basically two types of road graded as N (National) and R (Regional).

Sidelights should be used only when the vehicle is stationary in an unlit area. In the event of a breakdown the use of hazard warning lights or a warning triangle is compulsory, though warning triangles should not be used on motorways.

The blood alcohol limit is 80 mg per 100ml.

CAR FERRIES

Britanny Ferries www.brittanyferries.ie	Cork - Roscoff (summer only)	*021 4277801* **0870 9012400**
Irish Ferries www.irishferries.ie	Cork - Roscoff (summer only) Dublin - Holyhead Rosslare - Cherbourg (summer only) Rosslare - Pembroke Rosslare - Roscoff (summer only)	*1890 313131* **0800 0182211** **or 08705 171717**
Isle of Man Steam Packet Co. Ltd www.steam-packet.com	Belfast - Douglas (summer only) Dublin - Douglas (summer only)	*00441624 661661* **01624 661661**
Lough Foyle Ferry Co. Ltd	Greencastle (Inishowen) - Magilligan Point	*077 81901* **00353 7781901**
Norse Merchant Ferries www.norsemerchant.com	Belfast - Liverpool Dublin - Liverpool	*01 8192999* **0870 6004321**
P & O Irish Sea www.poirishsea.com	Dublin - Cherbourg (summer only) Dublin - Liverpool Dublin - Mostyn Quay Larne - Cairnryan Larne - Fleetwood Larne - Troon Rosslare - Cherbourg	*01 8557001* **0870 2424777**
SeaCat www.steam-packet.com	Belfast - Heysham (summer only) Belfast - Troon Dublin - Liverpool	*1800 551743* **08705 523523**
Stena Line www.stenaline.co.uk	Belfast - Stranraer Dublin - Holyhead Dún Laoghaire - Holyhead Rosslare - Fishguard	*01 2047700* **08705 707070**
Swansea Cork Ferries www.swansea-cork.ie	Cork - Swansea	*021 4271166* **01792 45611**

AIRPORTS

Belfast City (domestic) www.belfastcityairport.com	*(048)* **(028)** 9045 7745
Belfast International www.bial.co.uk	*(048)* **(028)** 9448 4848
City of Derry www.cityofderryairport.com	*(048)* **(028)** 7181 0784
Connemara (domestic)	*(091)* **(0035391)** 593034
Cork www.cork-airport.com	*(021)* **(0035321)** 4313131
Dublin www.dublin-airport.com	*(01)* **(003531)** 8141111
Galway (domestic) www.galwayairport.com	*(091)* **(0035391)** 755569
Kerry (domestic) www.kerryairport.ie	*(066)* **(0035366)** 9764644
Knock International www.knockinternationalairport.ie	*(094)* **(0035394)** 67222
Shannon www.shannonairport.com	*(061)* **(0035361)** 712000
Waterford homepage.tinet.ie/~wra	*(051)* **(0035351)** 875589

If telephoning from within the Republic of Ireland use *Italic* prefix/telephone number. If telephoning from Great Britain or Northern Ireland use **Bold** prefix/telephone number.

DISTANCE CHART

The distance between two selected towns will be found at the intersection of the respective vertical and horizontal rows, e.g. distance between Belfast and Dublin is 102 miles. In general, distances are based on the shortest routes by classified roads. Where a route includes a ferry journey, the mileage is shown in *italics*.

To find the approximate distance in kilometres multiply the mileage amount by 1.6.

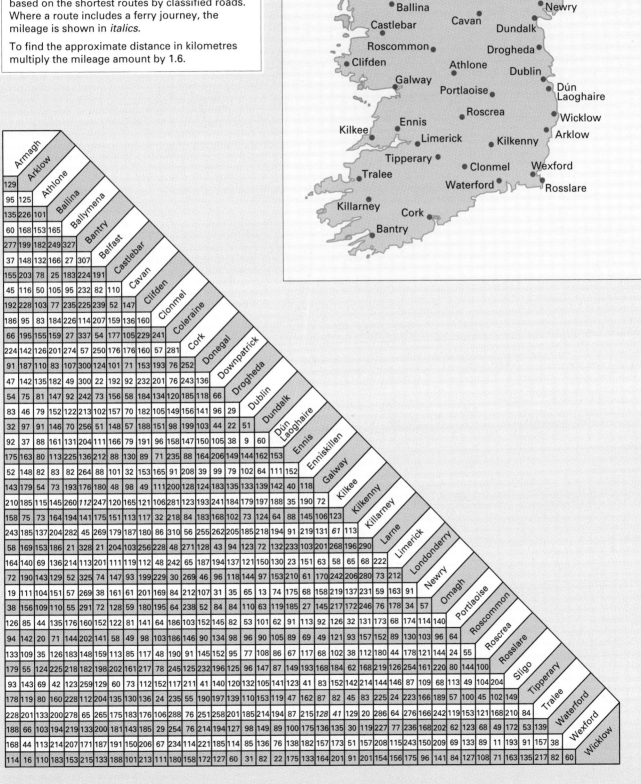

	Armagh	Arklow	Athlone	Ballina	Ballymena	Bantry	Belfast	Castlebar	Cavan	Clifden	Clonmel	Coleraine	Cork	Donegal	Downpatrick	Drogheda	Dublin	Dundalk	Dún Laoghaire	Ennis	Enniskillen	Galway	Kilkee	Kilkenny	Killarney	Larne	Limerick	Londonderry	Newry	Omagh	Portlaoise	Roscommon	Roscrea	Rosslare	Sligo	Tipperary	Tralee	Waterford	Wexford
Arklow	129																																						
Athlone	95	125																																					
Ballina	135	226	101																																				
Ballymena	60	168	153	165																																			
Bantry	277	199	182	249	327																																		
Belfast	37	148	132	166	27	307																																	
Castlebar	155	203	78	25	183	224	191																																
Cavan	45	116	50	105	95	232	82	110																															
Clifden	192	228	103	77	235	225	239	52	147																														
Clonmel	186	95	83	184	226	114	207	159	136	160																													
Coleraine	66	195	155	159	27	337	54	177	105	229	241																												
Cork	224	142	126	201	274	57	250	176	176	160	57	281																											
Donegal	91	187	110	83	107	300	124	101	71	153	193	76	252																										
Downpatrick	47	142	135	182	49	300	22	192	92	232	201	76	243	136																									
Drogheda	54	75	81	147	92	242	73	156	58	184	134	120	185	118	66																								
Dublin	83	46	79	152	122	213	102	157	70	182	105	149	156	141	96	29																							
Dundalk	32	97	91	146	70	256	51	148	57	188	151	98	199	103	44	22	51																						
Dún Laoghaire	92	37	88	161	131	204	111	166	79	191	96	158	147	150	105	38	9	60																					
Ennis	175	163	80	113	225	136	212	88	130	89	71	235	88	164	206	149	144	162	153																				
Enniskillen	52	148	82	83	82	264	88	101	32	153	165	91	208	39	99	79	102	64	111	152																			
Galway	143	179	54	73	193	176	180	48	98	49	111	200	128	124	183	135	133	139	142	40	118																		
Kilkee	210	185	115	145	260	*112*	247	120	165	121	106	281	123	193	241	184	179	197	188	35	190	72																	
Kilkenny	158	75	73	164	194	141	175	151	113	117	32	218	84	183	168	102	73	124	64	88	145	106	123																
Killarney	243	185	137	204	282	45	269	179	187	180	86	310	56	255	262	205	185	218	194	91	219	131	*61*	113															
Larne	58	169	153	186	21	328	21	204	103	256	228	48	271	128	43	94	123	72	132	233	103	201	268	196	290														
Limerick	164	140	69	136	214	113	201	111	119	112	48	242	65	187	194	137	121	150	130	23	151	63	58	65	68	222													
Londonderry	72	190	143	129	52	325	74	147	93	199	229	30	269	46	96	118	144	97	153	210	61	170	242	206	280	73	212												
Newry	19	111	104	151	57	269	38	161	61	201	169	84	212	107	31	35	65	13	74	175	68	158	219	137	231	59	163	91											
Omagh	38	156	109	110	55	291	72	128	59	180	195	64	238	52	84	84	110	63	119	185	27	145	217	172	246	76	178	34	57										
Portlaoise	126	85	44	135	176	160	152	122	81	141	64	186	103	152	145	82	53	101	62	91	113	92	126	32	131	173	68	174	114	140									
Roscommon	94	142	20	71	144	202	141	58	49	98	103	186	146	90	134	98	96	90	105	89	69	49	121	93	157	152	89	130	103	96	64								
Roscrea	133	109	35	126	183	148	159	113	85	117	48	190	91	145	152	95	77	108	86	67	117	68	102	38	112	180	44	178	121	144	24	55							
Rosslare	179	55	124	225	218	182	198	202	161	217	78	245	125	232	196	125	96	147	87	149	193	168	184	62	168	219	126	254	161	220	80	144	100						
Sligo	93	143	69	42	123	259	129	60	73	112	152	117	211	41	140	120	132	105	141	123	41	83	152	142	214	144	146	87	109	68	113	49	104	204					
Tipperary	178	119	80	160	228	112	204	135	130	136	24	235	55	190	197	139	110	153	119	47	162	87	82	45	83	225	24	223	166	189	57	100	45	102	149				
Tralee	228	201	133	200	278	65	265	175	183	176	106	288	76	251	258	201	185	214	194	87	215	*128*	*41*	129	20	286	64	276	166	242	119	153	121	168	210	84			
Waterford	188	66	103	194	219	133	200	181	143	185	29	254	76	214	194	127	98	149	89	100	175	136	135	30	119	227	77	236	168	202	62	123	68	49	172	53	139		
Wexford	168	44	113	214	207	171	187	191	150	206	67	234	114	221	185	114	85	136	76	138	182	157	173	51	157	208	115	243	150	209	69	133	89	11	193	91	157	38	
Wicklow	114	16	110	183	153	215	133	188	101	213	111	180	158	172	127	60	31	82	22	175	133	164	201	91	201	154	156	175	96	141	84	127	108	71	163	135	217	82	60

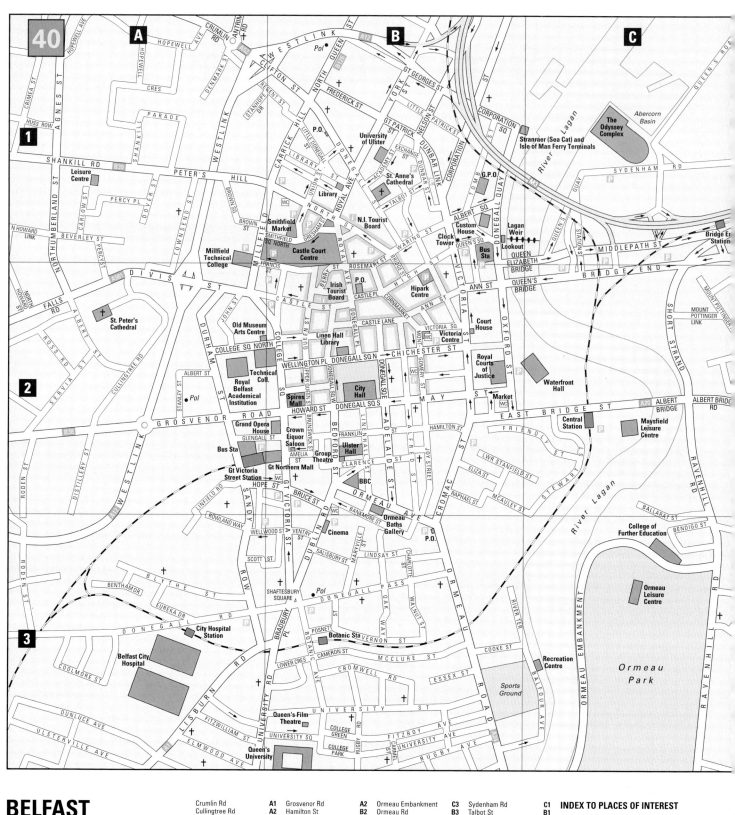

BELFAST

1:12,600 5 inches to 1 mile / 7.9 cm to 1 km

0   1/4 mile
0   1/4   1/2 kilometre

INDEX TO STREET NAMES

INDEX TO PLACES OF INTEREST

BELFAST INFORMATION

BRIEF HISTORY

Situated on the River Lagan, Belfast has a long and historic past. The city grew from a small village during the industrial revolution, with industries such as linen, rope making and ship building being major contributors. In fact the ship building industry still has an impact on Belfast, as the world's largest dry dock can be found here. In addition to this, Belfast holds another claim to fame from its shipbuilding, probably the world's most famous ship was built here, the Titanic.

There has been a period of regeneration in recent years, the city's riverfront area has been transformed and a major new concert venue, Waterfront Hall, has been built.

TOURIST INFORMATION CENTRE

The Welcome Centre
47 Donegall Place
BELFAST
BT1 5AD

(028) 9024 6609

GETTING AROUND

Two bus services run in and around the the city. The 'blue' Ulsterbuses, which transport people in and out of the city and the 'red' Citybuses which run within the city. Translink run the train services and both bus services.

Citybus   (028) 9024 6485
Ulsterbus   (028) 9033 3000
Northern Ireland Railways   (028) 9089 9411

GOLF COURSES (18 Hole)

Balmoral Golf Course
Belvoir Golf Course
Dunmurry Golf Course

Fortwilliam Golf Course
Knock Golf Course
Malone Golf Course

Mount Ober Golf & Country Club
Rockmount Golf Course
Shandon Park Golf Course

PLACES OF INTEREST

City Hall
Clock Tower
Custom House
Grand Opera House

Group Theatre
Lagan Weir & Lookout
Linen Hall Library
Lyric Theatre

St. Anne's Cathedral
St. Peter's Cathedral
Ulster Hall
Waterfront Hall

SHOPPING & LEISURE

Castle Court Centre
Great Northern Mall
Hipark Centre
Maysfield Leisure Centre
Smithfield Market
Spires Mall
Victoria Centre

TELEPHONING

If telephoning from Great Britain or Northern Ireland use the area code and telephone number. If telephoning from the Republic of Ireland use the code 00 44, delete the 0 from the area code and follow with the required telephone number, [e.g. (028) 9024 6609 in G.B. or Northern Ireland becomes (00 44 28) 9024 6609 in Republic of Ireland], or replace the area code with 048 [e.g. (028) 9024 6609 becomes (048) 9024 6609].

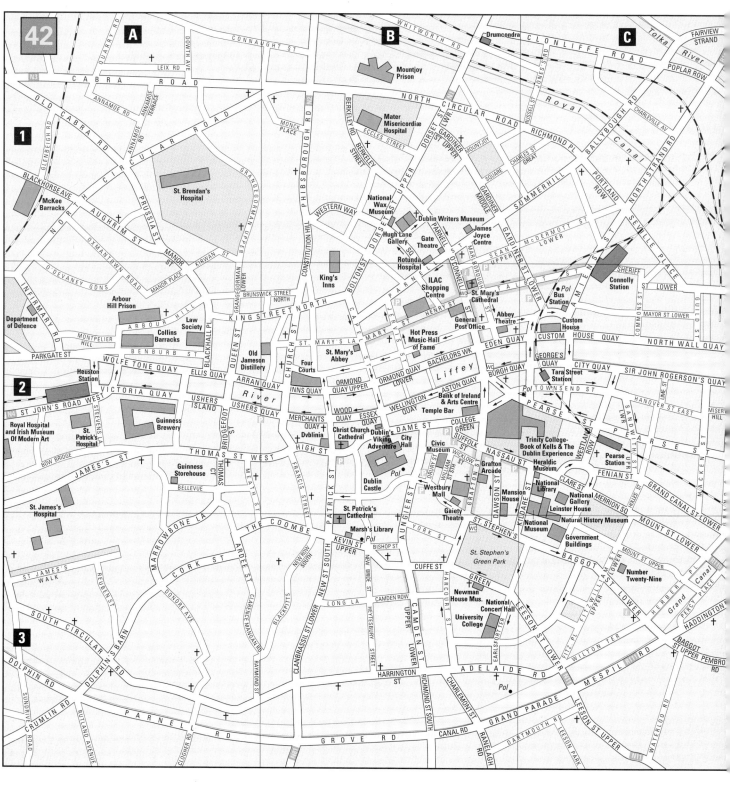

DUBLIN

0   1/4   1/2 mile

0   0.25   0.5   0.75   1 kilometre

1:19,000 (approx) 3.3 inches to 1 mile / 5.25 cm to 1 kilometre

DUBLIN INFORMATION

BRIEF HISTORY

Dublin is not only the capital city of the Republic of Ireland but also of County Dublin. It is situated near the coast of Dublin Bay, and the city straddles the River Liffey. Dublin derives its name from the old gaelic word Dubh Linn, meaning Black Pool. Over time this became the name that we now know, Dublin.

Dublin boasts the largest enclosed park in Europe, close to the city centre, Phoenix Park.

Dublin has produced many famous writers throughout history, some of which include, William Butler Yeats, George Bernard Shaw, Samuel Beckett and Bram Stoker, who wrote Dracula.

TOURIST INFORMATION OFFICES

Information Line . . . . 1850 230 330 (Republic of Ireland)
08000 397000 (G.B. & N.Ireland)
Accommodation Res. . . . . 1800 668 668 (Republic of Ireland)
00800 6686 6866 (G.B. & N.Ireland)

Walk In Offices
Suffolk Street, Dublin 2
O'Connell Street, Dublin 1
Dun Laoghaire Ferry Terminal
Arrivals Hall, Dublin Airport
Baggot Street Bridge, Dublin 2
The Square, Tallaght, Dublin 24

GETTING AROUND

All information on transport in and around Dublin can be obtained from
Córas Iompair Éireann (CIE)
59 O'Connell Street Upper
Dublin, 1
(01) 836 6111

GOLF COURSES (18 Hole)

Castle Golf Course
Clontarf Golf Course

Elm Park Golf Club
Forrest Little Golf Course

Milltown Golf Course
Royal Dublin Golf Course

PLACES OF INTEREST

Arbour Hill Prison
Book of Kells
Christ Church Cathedral
City Hall
Collins Barracks
Custom House
Dublin Castle
Dublin's Viking Adventure
Dublin's Writers Museum
Dvblinia
Guinness Storehouse

Heraldic Museum
Hugh Lane Gallery
Kings Inns
Leinster House
Mansion House
Marsh's Library
McKee Barracks
Mountjoy Prison
National Concert Hall
National Gallery
National Museum

National Wax Museum
Natural History Museum
Newman House Museum
Number Twenty Nine
Old Jameson Distillery
St. Mary's Pro-Cathedral
St. Patrick's Cathedral
St. Stephen's Green Park
The Dublin Experience
Trinity College

SHOPPING

Grafton Street
Henry Street/Talbot Street

Jervis Street
St. Stephen's Green

Temple Bar
Westbury Mall
(off Grafton Street)

TELEPHONING

If telephoning from Republic of Ireland use area code and telephone number. If telephoning from Great Britain or within Northern Ireland use the code 00 353, delete the 0 from the area code and follow with the required telephone number.
[e.g. (01) 836 6111 in Republic of Ireland becomes (00 353 1) 836 6111 from G.B. or Northern Ireland]

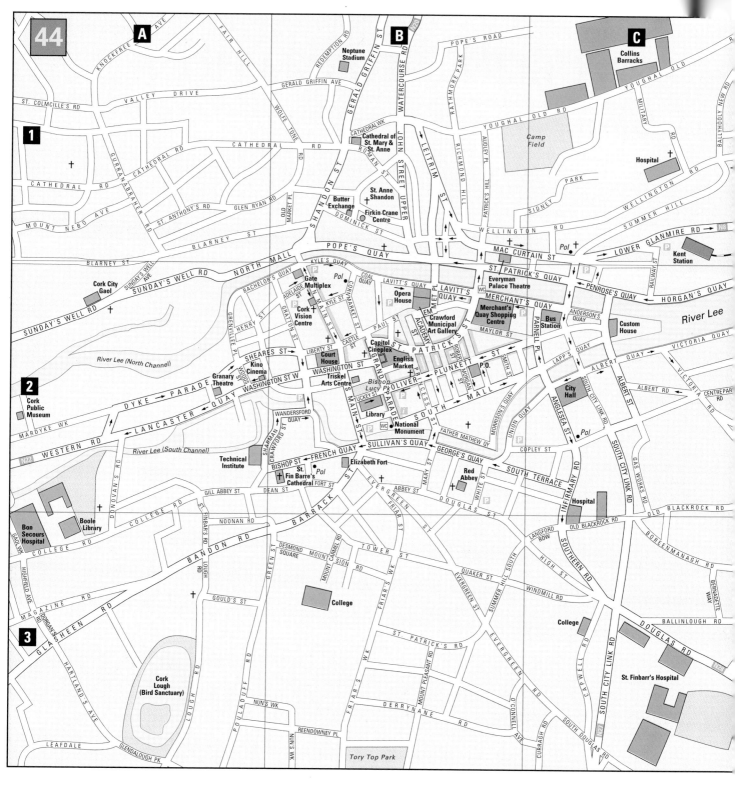

CORK

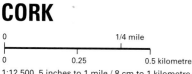

0   1/4 mile

0   0.25   0.5 kilometre

1:12,500   5 inches to 1 mile / 8 cm to 1 kilometre

INDEX TO STREET NAMES

44

A   B   C

1   2   3

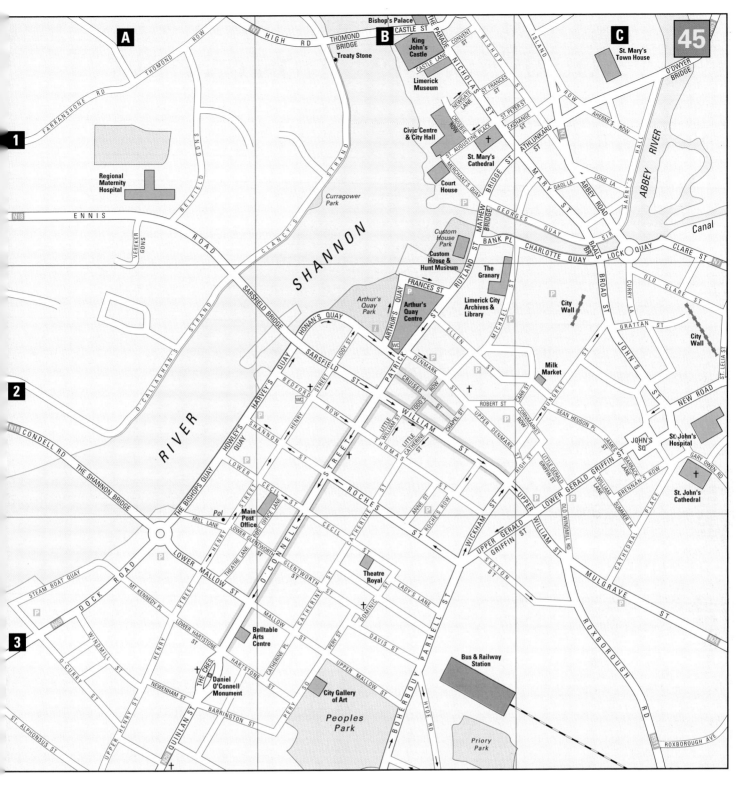

LIMERICK

1/4 mile

0.25 km

7,700 (approx) 8.2 inches to 1 mile / 13 cm to 1 km

INDEX TO STREET NAMES

herne's Row	C1	Chapel St	B2	Georges Quay	B1
nne St	B2	Charlotte Quay	C1	Glentworth St	B3
rthur's Quay	B2	Clancy's Strand	B1	Grattan St	C2
thlunkard St	C1	Clare St	C1	Hartstone St	A3
aals Bridge	C1	Condell Rd	A2	Harvey's Quay	A2
ank Pl	B1	Convent St	B1	Henry St	A3
arrack La	C2	Cornmarket Row	C2	High Rd	B1
arrington St	A3	Crosbie Row	B1	High St	C2
edford Row	B2	Cruises St	B2	Honan's Quay	B2
elfield Gdns	A1	Curry La	C2	Howley's Quay	A2
ishop St	B1	Davis St	B3	Hyde Rd	B3
oherbouy	B3	Denmark St	B2	Island Row	C1
rennan's Row	C2	Dock Rd	A3	James St	C2
ridge St	B1	Dominic St	B3	John's Sq	C2
road St	C2	Ellen St	B2	John's St	C2
arr St	C2	Ennis Rd	A1	Lady's La	B3
astle St	B1	Exchange St	B1	Liddy St	B2
athedral Pl	C3	Farranshone Rd	A1	Little Catherine St	B2
atherine Pl	B3	Frances St	B2	Little Gerald Griffin St	C2
atherine St	B3	Gaol La	C1	Little William St	B2
ecil St	B3	Gary Owen Rd	C2	Lock Quay	C1

Long La	C1	Robert St	B2	Upper Mallow St	B3
Lower Cecil St	A2	Roches Row	B3	Upper William St	C2
Lower Gerald Griffin St	C2	Roches St	B2	Vereker Gdns	A1
Lower Glentworth St	A3	Roxborough Av	C3	Wickham St	B3
Lower Hartstone St	A3	Roxborough Rd	C3	William La	C2
Lower Mallow St	A3	Rutland St	B2	William St	B2
Mallow St	B3	Sarsfield Bridge	A2	Windmill St	A3
Mary St	C1	Sarsfield St	B2	
Mathew Bridge	B1	Sean Heuson Pl	C2	
Merchant's Quay	B1	Sexton St	B3	
Michael St	B2	Shannon St	A2	
Mill La	A3	Sir Harry's Hall	C1	
Mt Kennedy Pl	A3	St. Alphonsus St	A3	
Mulgrave St	C3	St. Augustine Pl	B1	
Mungret St	C2	St. Frances St	B1	
New Rd	C2	St. Lelia St	C2	
Newenham St	A3	St. Peter St	B1	
Newgate La	B1	Steam Boat Quay	A3	
Nicholas St	B1	Summer La	C2	
O'Callaghan's Strand	A2	The Bishops Quay	A2	
O'Connell St	A3	The Crescent	A3	
O'Curry St	A3	The Parade	B1	
O'Dwyer Bridge	C1	The Shannon Bridge	A2	
Old Clare St	C2	Theatre La	B2	
Old Windmill Rd	C2	Thomas St	B2	
Parnell St	B3	Thomond Bridge	B1	
Patrick St	B2	Thomond Row	A1	
Pery Sq	B3	Todd's Row	B2	
Pery St	B3	Upper Denmark St	C2	
Post Office La	B3	Upper Gerald Griffin St	B3	
Quinlan St	A3	Upper Henry St	A3	

INDEX TO PLACES OF INTEREST

Arthur's Quay Centre	B2	Main Post Office	B2
Arthur's Quay Park	B2	Milk Market	C2
Belltable Arts Centre	A3	Peoples Park	B3
Bishop's Palace	B1	Priory Park	B3
Bus & Railway Station	B3	Regional Maternity	A1
City Gallery of Art	B3	Hospital	
City Wall	C2	St. John's Cathedral	C2
Civic Centre & City Hall	B1	St. John's Hospital	C2
Court House	B1	St. Mary's Cathedral	B1
Curragower Park	B1	St. Mary's Town House	C1
Custom House	B1	Theatre Royal	B3
Custom House Park	B1	The Granary	B2
Daniel O'Connell	A3	Treaty Stone	B1
Monument			
Hunt Museum	B1		
King John's Castle	B1		
Limerick City Archives	B2		
& Library			
Limerick Museum	B1		

TOURIST INFORMATION CENTRES

✻ Summer opening only

NORTHERN IRELAND

Area codes are for Great Britain and Northern Ireland

Antrim, Co. Antrim	16 High Street	☎ 028 9442 8331	13 C3
Armagh, Co. Armagh	Old Bank Building, 40 English Street	☎ 028 3752 1800	16 B3
Ballycastle, Co. Antrim	Sheskburn House, 7 Mary Street	☎ 028 2076 2024	13 C1
Ballymena, Co. Antrim	76 Church Street	☎ 028 2563 8494	13 C3
Banbridge, Co. Down	Gateway Tourist Information Centre, 200 Newry Road	☎ 028 4062 3322	17 C3
Bangor, Co. Down	34 Quay Street	☎ 028 9127 0069	17 D2
Belfast, Co. Antrim	Belfast Welcome Centre, Donegall Place	☎ 028 9024 6609	17 C2
Belfast, Co. Antrim	N.I. Tourist Board, 59 North Street	☎ 028 9023 1221	17 C2
Belfast, Co. Antrim	Irish Tourist Board, Castle Street	☎ 028 9032 7888	17 C2
Carrickfergus, Co. Antrim	Heritage Plaza, Antrim Street	☎ 028 9336 6455	13 D3
Coleraine, Co. Londonderry	Railway Road	☎ 028 7034 4723	12 B2
Cookstown, Co. Tyrone	The Burnavan, Burn Road	☎ 028 8676 6727	16 B2
Downpatrick, Co. Down	74 Market Street	☎ 028 4461 2233	17 D3
Enniskillen, Co. Fermanagh	Fermanagh Tourist Information Centre, Wellington Rd	☎ 028 6632 3110	15 D2
Giant's Causeway, Co. Antrim	44 Causeway Road, Bushmills	☎ 028 2073 1855	12 B1
Hillsborough, Co. Down	The Courthouse, The Square	☎ 028 9268 9717	17 C2
Kilkeel, Co. Down	28 Bridge Street	☎ 028 4176 2525	21 C1
Killymaddy, Co. Tyrone	Ballygawley Road, Dungannon	☎ 028 8776 7259	16 A2
Larne, Co. Antrim	Narrow Gauge Road	☎ 028 2826 0088	13 D3
Limavady, Co. Londonderry	Council Offices, 7 Connell Street	☎ 028 7776 0307	12 A2
Lisburn, Co. Antrim	Irish Linen Centre, Market Square	☎ 028 9266 0038	17 C2
Londonderry, Co. Londonderry	44 Foyle Street	☎ 028 7126 7284	11 D2
Newcastle, Co. Down	The Newcastle Centre, 10 - 14 Central Promenade	☎ 028 4372 2222	17 D3
Newtownards, Co. Down	31 Regent Street, Newtownards	☎ 028 9182 6846	17 D2
Omagh, Co. Tyrone	1 Market Street	☎ 028 8224 7831	15 D1
Portrush, Co. Antrim	Dunluce Centre, Sandhill Drive	☎ 028 7082 3333	12 B1
Strabane, Co. Tyrone	Abercorn Square	☎ 028 9288 3735	11 D3

REPUBLIC OF IRELAND

Area Codes are for Republic of Ireland

✻Achill, Co. Mayo	Cashel, Achill Island	☎ 098 45384	18 A2
✻Adare, Co. Limerick	Heritage Centre, Main Street	☎ 061 396255	28 A3
✻Aran Islands, Co. Galway	Kilronan, Inishmore, Aran Islands	☎ 099 61263	24 B3
✻Ardmore, Co. Waterford		☎ 024 94444	35 C2
✻Arklow, Co. Wicklow	Main Street	☎ 0402 32484	33 D1
✻Athlone, Co. Westmeath	Athlone Castle, St Peters Square	☎ 0902 94630	23 C2
✻Ballina, Co. Mayo	Cathedral Road	☎ 096 70848	19 C2
✻Ballinasloe, Co. Galway	Keller Travel, Main Street	☎ 0905 42131	22 B3
✻Ballinrobe, Co. Mayo	Cornmarket	☎ 092 42150	25 C1
✻Bantry, Co. Cork	The Old Courthouse, The Square	☎ 027 50229	37 C2
✻Birr, Co. Offaly	Castle Street	☎ 0509 20110	29 C1
Blarney, Co. Cork		☎ 021 4381624	34 A2
✻Boyle, Co. Roscommon		☎ 079 62145	14 B3
Brú Na Bóinne, Co. Meath	Donore	☎ 041 9880 305	20 B2
✻Buncrana, Co. Donegal	Railway Road	☎ 077 62600	11 D2
Bundoran, Co. Donegal	The Bridge	☎ 072 41350	14 B1
✻Cahirciveen, Co. Kerry	RIC Barracks	☎ 066 9472589	36 A1
✻Cahir, Co. Tipperary		☎ 052 41453	29 C3
Carlingford, Co. Louth	Dispensary Building	☎ 042 937 3033	21 C1
Carlow, Co. Carlow	Tullow Street	☎ 0503 32554	32 B1
Carrick-on-Shannon, Co. Leitrim	The Marina	☎ 078 20170	14 B3
Carrick-on-Suir, Co. Tipperary	Heritage Centre	☎ 051 640200	32 A2
✻Cashel, Co. Tipperary	Main Street	☎ 062 61333	29 C3
✻Castlebar, Co. Mayo	Linenhall Street	☎ 094 21207	19 C3
Cavan, Co. Cavan	Farnham Street	☎ 049 4331942	15 D3
✻Clifden, Co. Galway	Market Street	☎ 095 21163	24 A1
✻Cliffs of Moher, Co. Clare	Liscannor	☎ 065 7081171	24 B3
Clonakilty, Co. Cork	25 Ashe Street	☎ 023 33226	34 A3
✻Clonmacnoise, Co. Offaly		☎ 0905 74134	23 C3
Clonmel, Co. Tipperary	6 Sarsfield Street	☎ 052 22960	35 C1
✻Cong, Co. Mayo	Abbey Street	☎ 092 46542	25 C1
✻Cork City, Co Cork	Tourist House, Grand Parade	☎ 021 4255100	34 B2
Dingle, Co. Kerry	The Pier	☎ 066 9151188	30 A3
✻Donegal Town, Co. Donegal	The Quay	☎ 073 21148	14 B1
Drogheda, Co. Louth	Bus Station, Donore Road	☎ 041 9837070	21 C2
Dublin Airport, Co. Dublin	Arrivals Hall, Dublin Airport	☎ 1850 230 330	27 D2

Dublin City, Co. Dublin, Tourist Information	14 Upper O'Connell Street (R.O.I.)	☎ 1850 230 330	**27 D2**
	(U.K.)	☎ (020)74933201	
Dublin Credit Card Reservations	(R.O.I.)	☎ 1800 668 668	**27 D2**
	(U.K.)	☎ 00800 668 668 66	
Dublin City, Co. Dublin	Baggot Street Bridge	☎ 1850 230 330	**27 D2**
Dublin City, Co. Dublin	Suffolk Street	☎ 1850 230 330	**27 D2**
Dublin City, Co. Dublin	New Ferry Terminal, Dún Laoghaire	☎ 1850 230 330	**27 D2**
Dublin City, Co. Dublin	The Square, Tallaght	☎ 1850 230 330	**27 D2**
Dundalk, Co. Louth	Jocelyn Street	☎ 042 9335484	**20 B1**
Dungarvan, Co. Waterford	Gratton Square	☎ 058 41741	**35 D2**
⁕Dungloe, Co. Donegal	Main Street	☎ 075 21297	**10 B2**
Ennis, Co. Clare	Arthurs Row	☎ 065 6828366	**31 D1**
⁕Enniscorthy, Co. Wexford		☎ 054 34699	**33 C2**
Fethard, Co. Tipperary	Tierry Centre	☎ 052 31000	**29 C3**
Galway, Co. Galway	Aras Failte, Forster Street	☎ 091 537700	**25 C2**
⁕Glendalough, Co. Wicklow	Upper Lake	☎ 0404 45425	**27 D3**
⁕Glengarriff, Co. Cork	Eccles Car Park	☎ 027 63084	**37 C2**
Gorey, Co. Wexford	Market House, Main Street	☎ 055 21248	**33 D1**
⁕Hook Head, Co. Wexford		☎ 051 397502	**32 B3**
⁕Kenmare, Co. Kerry	Heritage Centre	☎ 064 41233	**37 C1**
Kildare, Co. Kildare	Market Square	☎ 045 521240	**26 B2**
⁕Kilkee, Co. Clare	The Square	☎ 065 9056112	**31 C2**
Kilkenny, Co. Kilkenny	Shee Alms House, Rose Inn Street	☎ 056 51500	**32 A1**
⁕Killaloe, Co. Clare	Heritage Centre	☎ 061 376866	**28 B2**
Killarney, Co. Kerry	Beech Road	☎ 064 31633	**37 C1**
⁕Kilrush, Co. Clare	Town Hall	☎ 065 9051577	**31 C1**
Kinsale, Co. Cork	Pier Road	☎ 021 4772234	**34 A3**
⁕Knock, Co. Mayo		☎ 094 88193	**19 D3**
⁕Knock International Airport, Co. Mayo	Charlestown	☎ 094 67247	**19 D2**
Letterkenny, Co. Donegal	Neil T. Blaney Road	☎ 074 21160	**11 C2**
Limerick City, Co. Limerick	Arthur's Quay	☎ 061 317522	**28 A3**
⁕Lismore, Co. Waterford	Lismore Heritage Centre	☎ 058 54975	**35 C1**
⁕Listowel, Co. Kerry	St. John's Church, The Square	☎ 068 22590	**31 C2**
Longford, Co. Longford	Dublin Street	☎ 043 46566	**23 C1**
⁕Macroom, Co. Cork	Castle Gates, The Square	☎ 026 43280	**37 D1**
⁕Midleton, Co. Cork	Jameson Heritage Centre, Distillery Walk	☎ 021 4613702	**34 B2**
Monaghan, Co. Monaghan	Market House	☎ 047 81122	**16 A3**
Mullingar, Co. Westmeath	Market House	☎ 044 48650 & 48761	**23 D2**
⁕Navan, Co. Meath	Ludlow Street	☎ 046 73426	**20 B2**
⁕Nenagh, Co. Tipperary	Connolly Street	☎ 067 31610	**28 B2**
⁕Newport, Co. Mayo		☎ 098 41895	**18 B3**
⁕New Ross, Co. Wexford		☎ 051 421857	**32 B2**
⁕Oranmore, Co. Galway		☎ 091 790811	**25 D2**
Oughterard, Co. Galway	Main Street	☎ 091 552808	**25 C1**
Portlaoise, Co. Laois	James Fintan Lawlor Avenue	☎ 0502 21178	**29 D1**
⁕Roscommon, Co. Roscommon		☎ 0903 26342	**22 B2**
Rosslare Terminal, Co. Wexford	Kilrane	☎ 053 33232	**33 D3**
⁕Salthill, Co. Galway		☎ 091 520500	**25 C2**
Shannon Airport, Co. Clare	Arrivals Hall	☎ 061 471664	**28 A2**
Skibbereen, Co. Cork	Town Hall	☎ 028 21766	**37 D3**
Sligo, Co. Sligo	Áras Reddan, Temple Street	☎ 071 61201	**14 B2**
⁕Thoor Ballylee, Co. Galway	Thoor Ballylee, Gort	☎ 091 631436	**25 D3**
Tipperary, Co. Tipperary	EXCEL Centre	☎ 062 51457	**28 B3**
Tralee, Co. Kerry	Ashe Hall, Denny Street	☎ 066 7121288	**31 C3**
⁕Tramore, Co. Waterford		☎ 051 381572	**32 B3**
⁕Trim, Co. Meath	Mill Street	☎ 046 37111	**20 B3**
⁕Tuam, Co. Galway	The Mill Museum, Tuam	☎ 093 25486	**25 D1**
Tullamore, Co. Offaly	Tullamore Dew Heritage Centre, Bury Quay	☎ 0506 52617	**23 D3**
Waterford, Co. Waterford	The Granary, Merchants Quay	☎ 051 875823	**32 B3**
Waterford, Co. Waterford	Waterford Crystal Visitor Centre, Cork Road	☎ 051 358397	**32 B3**
⁕Waterville, Co. Kerry		☎ 066 947 4646	**36 A2**
Westport, Co. Mayo	James Street	☎ 098 25711	**18 B3**
Wexford, Co. Wexford	Crescent Quay	☎ 053 23111	**33 C3**
Wicklow, Co. Wicklow	Rialto House, Fitzwilliam Square	☎ 0404 69117	**27 D3**

INDEX TO PLACE NAMES

Place	Pg	Ref	Place	Pg	Ref	Place	Pg	Ref	Place	Pg	Ref
Kilwaughter	13	C3	Leenane	24	B1	Louth	20	B1	Millbrook	20	A2
Kilworth	34	B1	Leggs	15	C1	Lower Ballinderry	17	C2	Millford	16	B3
Kilworth Camp	34	B1	Leighlinbridge	32	B1	Lucan	27	C2	Millisle	17	D2
Kincon	19	C1	Leitrim *Down*	17	C3	Lukeswell	32	B2	Millstreet *Cork*	37	D1
Kindrum	11	C1	Leitrim *Leitrim*	15	C3	Lullymore	26	B2	Millstreet *Waterford*	35	C1
Kingarrow	11	C3	Leixlip	27	C2	Lurgan *Armagh*	16	B2	Milltown *Cavan*	15	D3
Kingscourt	20	A1	Lemybrien	35	D1	Lurgan *Roscommon*	22	B1	Milltown *Down*	17	C3
Kingsland	14	B3	Lenan	11	D1	Lusk	21	C3	Milltown *Galway*	22	A2
Kinlough	14	B1	Lerrig	31	C2	Lyracrumpane	31	C2	Milltown *Kerry*	31	C3
Kinnadoohy	18	A3	Letterbarra	10	B3	Lyre	34	A2	Milltown *Kerry*	30	A3
Kinnegad	20	A3	Letterbreen	15	C2	Lyrenaglogh	34	B1	Milltown *Kildare*	26	B2
Kinnitty	29	C1	Lettercallow	24	B2				Milltown *Tyrone*	16	A2
Kinsale	34	A3	Letterfinish	36	B1	**M**			Milltown Malbay	31	C1
Kinsalebeg	35	C2	Letterfrack	24	A1	Maam	24	B1	Minane Bridge	34	B3
Kinvara	22	A3	Letterkenny	11	C2	Maam Cross	24	B1	Mine Head	35	D2
Kinvarra	24	B2	Lettermacaward	10	B3	Maas	10	B3	Minerstown	17	D3
Kircubbin	17	D2	Lettermullen	24	B2	MacGregor's Corner	13	C2	Mitchelstown	34	B1
Kishkeam	31	D3	Levally	22	A2	Macosquin	12	A3	Moate	23	C3
Knightstown	36	A1	Lifford	11	D3	Macroom	37	D1	Modreeny	29	C1
Knock *Clare*	31	C1	Limavady	12	A2	Maganey	26	B3	Mogeely	35	C2
Knock *Mayo*	22	A1	Limerick (Luimneach)	28	A2	Maghanlawaun	36	B1	Mohil	29	D2
Knock *Tipperary*	29	C1	Lisacul	22	A1	Maghera *Donegal*	10	A3	Mohill	15	C3
Knock International Airport	14	A3	Lisbane	17	D2	Maghera *Londonderry*	12	B3	Moira	17	C2
Knockaderry	31	D2	Lisbellaw	15	D2	Magherafelt	12	B3	Monaghan (Muineachán)	16	A3
Knockalough	31	D1	Lisburn	17	C2	Magheralin	17	C2	Monamolin	33	D2
Knockananna	27	C3	Liscannor	24	B3	Magheramason	11	D2	Monasterevan	26	B2
Knockanarrigan	27	C3	Liscarney	18	B3	Maghery *Armagh*	16	B2	Monea	15	C2
Knockanevin	34	B1	Liscarroll	34	A1	Maghery *Donegal*	10	B3	Moneen	22	A2
Knockbrack	11	C3	Liscolman	12	B2	Magilligan	12	A2	Moneydig	12	B2
Knockbrandon	33	C1	Lisdoonvarna	25	C3	Maguiresbridge	15	D2	Moneygall	29	C2
Knockbridge	20	B1	Lisdowney	29	D2	Mahoonagh	31	D2	Moneyglass	12	B3
Knockbrit	29	C3	Lisduff	20	A2	Mainham	27	C2	Moneylahan	14	B2
Knockcroghery	22	B2	Lisgarode	28	B1	Malahide	21	C3	Moneymore	12	B3
Knocklong	28	B3	Lisgoold	34	B2	Malin	11	D1	Moneyneany	12	A3
Knockmore	19	C2	Lislea	12	B3	Malin Beg	14	A1	Moneyreagh	17	D2
Knockmoyle	28	B1	Lismakin	29	C1	Malin More	10	A3	Monilea	23	D2
Knocknaboul	31	D3	Lismore	35	C1	Mallow (Mala)	34	A1	Monivea	22	A3
Knocknacarry	13	C2	Lisnageer	20	A1	Manorcunningham	11	D2	Montpelier	28	B2
Knocknacree	26	B3	Lisnagry	28	A2	Manorhamilton	14	B2	Mooncoin	35	D1
Knocknagashel	31	C3	Lisnakill	32	B3	Manseltown	29	C2	Moone	26	B3
Knocknagree	31	D3	Lisnamuck	12	B3	Manulla	19	C3	Moorfields	13	C3
Knocknalina	18	A1	Lisnarrick	15	C1	Markethill	16	B3	Morley's Bridge	37	C1
Knockraha	34	B2	Lisnaskea	15	D2	Marshalstown	33	C2	Moss-side	12	B2
Knocks	37	D2	Lispatrick	34	A3	Martinstown *Antrim*	13	C2	Mossley	13	C3
Knocktopher	32	B2	Lispole	30	B3	Martinstown *Limerick*	28	B3	Mothel	35	D1
			Lisrodden	12	B3	Massford	17	C3	Mount Bellew	22	B2
L			Lisronagh	29	C3	Masshill	14	A3	Mount Hamilton	12	A3
Laban	22	A3	Lisryan	23	D1	Mastergeehy	36	B1	Mount Norris	16	B3
Labasheeda	31	D1	Lissan	12	A3	Matehy	34	A2	Mount Nugent	23	D1
Lack	15	D1	Lissatinning Bridge	36	B1	Matry	20	A2	Mount Talbot	22	B2
Lackamore	28	B2	Lisselton	31	C2	Mauricemills	25	C3	Mountallen	15	C3
Lackan	23	D2	Lissiniska	14	B2	Maynooth	27	C2	Mountbolus	23	D3
Ladysbridge	35	C2	Lissycasey	31	D1	Mayo	19	C3	Mountcharles	14	B1
Lagavara	12	B1	Listerlin	32	B2	Mayobridge	17	C3	Mountcollins	31	D3
Laghey	14	B1	Listooder	17	D2	May's Corner	17	C3	Mountfield	16	A2
Laghtgeorge	22	A3	Listowel	31	C2	Meelick	22	B3	Mountjoy *Tyrone*	16	B2
Lahardaun	19	C2	Listry	31	C3	Meelin	31	D3	Mountjoy *Tyrone*	15	D1
Lahinch	25	C3	Littleton	29	C2	Meenaclady	10	B2	Mountmellick	29	D1
Lanesborough	23	C1	Lixnaw	31	C2	Meenacross	10	B3	Mountrath	29	D1
Laracor	20	B3	Lobinstown	20	B2	Meenanarwa	10	B3	Mountshannon	28	B1
Laragh	27	D3	Loghill	31	D2	Meenavean	14	A1	Moville	12	A1
Largan	14	A3	Londonderry (Derry)	11	D2	Meenglass	11	C3	Moy	16	B2
Larne	13	D3	Longford	23	C1	Meentullynagarn	10	B3	Moyard	24	A1
Lauragh	36	B2	Longwood	20	A3	Meigh	20	B1	Moyarget	12	B1
Laurencetown	22	B3	Loskeran	35	D2	Menlough	25	C2	Moyasta	31	C1
Lavagh	14	A3	Lough Gowna	23	D1	Middletown	16	A3	Moycullen	25	C2
Lawrencetown	17	C3	Loughanure	10	B2	Midfield	22	A1	Moydow	23	C1
Laytown	21	C2	Loughbrickland	17	C3	Midleton	34	B2	Moygashel	16	A2
Leabgarrow	10	B2	Lougher	30	B3	Mile House	33	C2	Moylaw	18	B2
Leamlara	34	B2	Loughgall	16	B3	Milebush	13	D3	Moylett	20	A1
Leap	37	D3	Loughglinn	22	A1	Milestone	28	B2	Moylough	22	A2
Lecarrow	23	C2	Loughinisland	17	D3	Milford *Cork*	34	A1	Moymore	28	A2
Leckaun	14	B2	Loughmoe	29	C2	Milford *Donegal*	11	C2	Moynalty	20	A2
			Loughrea	22	A3				Moyne *Longford*	15	D3
			Louisburgh	18	B3						

Moyne *Roscommon*	22	A1
Moyne *Wicklow*	33	C1
Moyrus	24	A2
Moys	12	A2
Moyvalley	20	A3
Moyvore	23	D2
Moyvoughly	23	C2
Mucklon	26	B2
Muckross	37	C1
Muff	11	D2
Muine Bheag	32	B1
Mullagh *Cavan*	20	A2
Mullagh *Clare*	31	C1
Mullagh *Mayo*	18	B3
Mullagh *Meath*	20	B3
Mullaghmore	14	B1
Mullaghroe	14	B3
Mullan *Fermanagh*	15	C2
Mullan *Monaghan*	16	A3
Mullany's Cross	14	A3
Mullartown	21	D1
Mullinahone	29	D3
Mullinavat	32	B3
Mullingar	23	D2
(Án Muileann gCearr)		
Mulrany	18	B2
Multyfarnham	23	D2
Mungret	28	A2
Murley	15	D2
Murntown	33	C3
Murrisk	18	B3
Murrooph	25	C2
Myshall	33	C1

N

Naas (An Nás)	27	C2
Nad	34	A2
Narin	10	B3
Naul	21	C3
Navan (Án Uaimh)	20	B3
Neale	24	B1
Nealstown	29	C1
Nenagh (An Aonach)	28	B2
New Birmingham	29	D3
New Buildings	11	D2
New Ferry	12	B3
New Inn *Cavan*	20	A2
New Inn *Galway*	22	B3
New Inn *Laois*	26	B3
New Kildimo	28	A3
New Ross	32	B2
Newbawn	33	C3
Newbliss	20	A1
Newbridge *Galway*	22	B2
Newbridge *Limerick*	31	D2
Newbridge (Droichead	27	C2
Nua) *Kildare*		
Newcastle *Down*	17	D3
Newcastle *Dublin*	27	C2
Newcastle *Galway*	22	A3
Newcastle *Tipperary*	35	C1
Newcastle *Wicklow*	27	D3
Newcastle West	31	D2
Newcestown	34	A3
Newgrange	20	B2
Newinn	29	C3
Newmarket *Cork*	31	D3
Newmarket *Kilkenny*	29	D3
Newmarket-on-Fergus	28	A2
Newport *Mayo*	18	B3
Newport *Tipperary*	28	B2
Newport Trench	16	B2
Newry	17	C3
Newtown *Cork*	34	A1

Newtown *Kildare*	20	B3
Newtown *Laois*	32	B1
Newtown *Meath*	20	B2
Newtown	22	B3
Roscommon		
Newtown *Tipperary*	29	C1
Newtown *Tipperary*	28	B3
Newtown *Waterford*	35	D1
Newtown Crommelin	13	C2
Newtown Forbes	23	C1
Newtown Gore	15	C3
Newtown Sandes	31	C2
Newtownabbey	13	C3
Newtownards	17	D2
Newtownbutler	15	D2
Newtowncashel	23	C2
Newtowncunningham	11	D2
Newtownhamilton	16	B3
Newtownlow	23	D3
Newtownlynch	25	C2
Newtownmount-	27	D3
kennedy		
Newtownstewart	11	D3
Ninemilehouse	29	D3
Nobber	20	B2
Nohoval	34	B3
North Ring	34	A3
Noughaval	25	C3
Nurney *Carlow*	32	B1
Nurney *Kildare*	26	B3
Nutt's Corner	17	C2

O

O'Briensbridge	28	A2
Ogonelloe	28	B1
Oilgate	33	C2
Old Head	34	A3
Old Leighlin	32	B1
Old Ross	32	B2
Old Town *Donegal*	11	C2
Old Town	23	C3
Roscommon		
Oldcastle	20	A2
Oldcourt	27	C2
Oldtown	21	C3
Omagh	15	D1
Omeath	21	C1
Onaght	24	A2
Oola	28	B3
Oran	22	B1
Oranmore	22	A3
Oristown	20	B2
Oughterard	25	C1
Oulart	33	D2
Ovens	34	A2
Owenbeg	14	A2
Oysterhaven	34	B3

P

Pallas Green	28	B3
Pallaskenry	28	A2
Palmerston	27	C2
Park	12	A3
Parkmore	25	C2
Parknasilla	36	B2
Partry	19	C3
Passage East	32	B3
Passage West	34	B2
Patrickswell	28	A3
Peterswell	28	A1
Pettigo	15	C1
Pharis	12	B2
Pipers Town	23	C1

Pluck	11	D2
Plumbridge	11	D3
Pollatomish	18	B1
Pomeroy	16	A2
Pontoon	19	C2
Port *Donegal*	10	A3
Port *Louth*	21	C2
Portacloy	18	B1
Portadown	16	B2
Portaferry	17	D3
Portaleen	12	A1
Portarlington	26	B2
Portavogie	17	D2
Portballintrae	12	B1
Portglenone	12	B3
Portland	28	B1
Portlaoise	29	D1
Portlaw	35	D1
Portmagee	36	A1
Portmarnock	21	C3
Portmuck	13	D3
Portnoo	10	B3
Portrane	21	C3
Portroe	28	B1
Portrush	12	B1
Portsalon	11	D1
Portstewart	12	B2
Portumna	28	B1
Porturlin	18	B1
Poulgorm Bridge	37	D1
Poulnamucky	29	C3
Power's Cross	28	B1
Poyntz Pass	16	B3
Priesthaggard	32	B3
Prosperous	27	C2
Puckaun	28	B1

Q

Querrin	31	C1
Quin	28	A2

R

Raffrey	17	D2
Raghly	14	A2
Rahan	23	D3
Raheen	34	A3
Ramelton	11	C2
Randalstown	12	B3
Rapemills	23	C3
Raphoe	11	D3
Rasharkin	12	B2
Rashedoge	11	C2
Rath	23	C3
Rathangan	26	B2
Rathcabban	29	C1
Rathconrath	23	D2
Rathcool	37	D1
Rathcoole	27	C2
Rathcor	21	C1
Rathcormac	34	B2
Rathdangan	27	C3
Rathdowney	29	D2
Rathdrum	27	D3
Rathfarnham	27	D2
Rathfriland	17	C3
Rathgormuck	35	D1
Rathkeale	31	D2
Rathkeevin	29	C3
Rathkenny	20	B2
Rathlackan	19	C1
Rathlee	19	C1
Rathluirc (Charleville)	34	A1
Rathmolyon	20	A3

Rathmore *Kerry*	37	D1
Rathmore *Kildare*	27	C2
Rathmullan	11	D2
Rathnew	27	D3
Rathnure	33	C2
Rathowen	23	D2
Rathumney	32	B3
Rathvilly	33	C1
Ratoath	20	B3
Ravensdale	21	C1
Reaghstown	20	B1
Reanaclogheen	35	C2
Reanagowan	31	C3
Reananeree	37	D1
Reanascreena	37	D2
Rear Cross	28	B2
Recess	24	B1
Redcastle	12	A2
Redcross	27	D3
Redhills	15	D3
Reen	37	C1
Reens	31	D2
Rerrin	36	B2
Rhode	26	B2
Richhill	16	B3
Ringaskiddy	34	B3
Ringsend	12	A3
Ringville	35	D2
Rinneen	24	B3
Rinvyle	24	A1
Riverchapel	33	D1
Riverstown *Cork*	34	B2
Riverstown *Sligo*	14	B3
Riverstown *Tipperary*	29	C1
Roadford	24	B3
Robertstown	26	B2
Rochestown	32	B3
Rochfortbridge	23	D2
Rockcorry	20	A1
Rockhill	28	A3
Rockmills	34	B1
Rooaun	23	C3
Rookchapel	31	D3
Roonah Quay	18	A3
Roosky *Mayo*	14	A3
Roosky *Roscommon*	23	C1
Rosapenna	11	C2
Rosbeg	10	A3
Rosbercon	32	B2
Roscommon	22	B2
Roscrea	29	C1
Rosegreen	29	C3
Rosenallis	29	D1
Rosmuck	24	B2
Ross	23	D1
Ross Carbery	37	D3
Rossaveel	24	B2
Rossbrin	37	C3
Rosscahill	25	C2
Rosscor	15	C1
Rosses Point	14	A2
Rossinver	14	B2
Rosslare	33	D3
Rosslare Harbour	33	D3
Rosslea	16	A3
Rossnowlagh	14	B1
Rostellan	34	B3
Rostrevor	21	C1
Rosturk	18	A3
Roundfort	25	C1
Roundstone	24	A1
Roundwood	27	D3
Rousky	12	A3
Ruan	25	C3
Rubane	17	D2

RADIO STATIONS

RADIO STATION	FREQUENCY	RECEIVING AREAS
NORTHERN IRELAND BBC RADIO STATIONS www.bbc.co.uk/radio		
Radio 1	97.9 - 99.7 FM	National
Radio 2	88.3 - 90.1 FM	National
Radio 3	90.5 - 96.0 FM	National
Radio 4	93.0 - 95.6, 103.5 -103.9 FM	National
Radio 5	693 , 909 AM	National
BBC World Service www.bbc.co.uk/worldservice	648	International
Radio Ulster www.bbc.co.uk/northernireland/radio	92.7 - 95.4, 104.6 FM 873, 1341 AM	Ulster
(Radio Foyle)	(93.1 FM 792 AM)	(Londonderry)
NORTHERN IRELAND INDEPENDENT RADIO STATIONS		
Classic FM www.classicfm.com	100.5, 101.9 FM	National
Talksport www.talksport.net	1053 , 1089 AM	National
Virgin Radio www.virginradio.co.uk	1215 AM	National
City Beat www.citybeat.co.uk	96.7 FM	Belfast
Cool FM www.coolfm.co.uk	97.4 FM	Belfast
Downtown Radio www.downtown.co.uk	1026 AM / 102.4 / 96.4 / 96.6 FM	Belfast / Londonderry / Limavady / Enniskillen
Gold Beat 828 AM	828 AM	Mid Ulster
Magic 105 www.magic105.net	101.5 / 105.1 / 105.8 FM	SE Ulster / Mid Ulster / Tyrone & Fermanagh
Q97.2FM Causeway Coast Radio www.q102.fm/97new	97.2 FM	Causeway Coast
Q101.2 West FM www.radiowest.fm	102.9 FM	Tyrone & Fermanagh
Q102.9FM www.q102.fm/102new	102.9 FM	Londonderry
REPUBLIC OF IRELAND RTÉ RADIO STATIONS		
2 FM www.2fm.ie	90 - 92, 97.0 FM, 612, 1278 AM	National
Lyric FM www.lyricfm.ie	96 - 99 FM	National
Radio 1 www.radio1.ie	88.2 - 90.0, 95.2 FM, 567, 729 AM	National
Raidió Na Gaeltachta www.rnag.ie	92.9 - 94.2, 102.7 FM	National
REPUBLIC OF IRELAND INDEPENDENT RADIO STATIONS		
98 FM www.98frm.ie	98.1 FM	Co. Dublin
Anna Livia FM	103.2 FM	Co. Dublin
CKR FM	97.3 / 97.6,107.4 FM	Co. Carlow / Kildare
Clare FM www.clarefm.ie	95.2, 95.5, 95.9, 96.2 FM	Co. Clare
Cork 96 FM / 103 FM County Sound www.96fm.ie	96.4 / 103.3 / 103.7 FM	Co. Cork
Dublins Country 106.8FM www.dublinscountry.com	106.8 FM	Dublin City
East Coast FM www.eastcoast.fm	94.9, 102.9 / 96.2, 104.4 FM	Co. Wicklow
FM 104 www.fm104.ie	104.4 FM	Co. Dublin
Galway Bay FM gbfm.galway.net	95.8, 96.0, 96.8, 97.4 FM	Co. Galway
Highland Radio www.highlandradio.com	87.9, 95.2, 103.3 FM	Co. Donegal (North)
Limericks Live 95 FM www.live95fm.ie	95.0, 95.3 FM	Co. Limerick
Lite 102.2 FM www.litefm.ie	102.2 FM	Co. Dublin
LM FM www.lmfm.ie	95.5, 95.8, 104.9 FM	Co. Louth
Midlands Radio 3 www.midlandsradio.fm	96.2, 96.5, 102.1, 103.5 FM	Co. Laois / Offaly / Westmeath
Mid West Radio FM www.mnwrfm.com	95.4, 96.1, 97.1, 97.2 FM	Co. Mayo
Newstalk 106FM www.newstalk106.ie	106 FM	Co. Dublin
Northern Sound Radio	94.8, 96.3, 97.5 FM	Co. Cavan / Monaghan
North West Radio www.mnwrfm.com	94.7, 102.5 / 105 FM	Co. Donegal / Sligo / N. Leitrim
Radio Kerry www.radiokerry.ie	96.2, 96.6, 97.0, 97.6 FM	Co. Kerry
Radio Kilkenny www.radiokilkenny.com	96.0, 96.6,106.3 FM	Co. Kilkenny
Raidió na Life www.iol.ie/~rnl102	106.4 FM	Co. Dublin
Red FM 104-106 www.redfm.ie	104-106 FM	Co. Cork
Shannonside 104 FM	95.7, 103.1, 104.1 FM	Co. Roscommon / Longford / Leitrim (South)
South East Radio www.southeastradio.ie	95.6, 96.2, 96.4 FM	Co. Wexford
Spin 103.8 FM www.spin1038.com	103.8 FM	Co. Dublin
Tipperary Mid West Radio	104.8 FM	Co. Tipperary (South West)
Tipp FM www.tippfm.com	95.3, 97.1, 103.9 FM	Co. Tipperary (South East & North)
Today FM www.todayfm.com	100 -101.8, 105.5 FM	National
WLR FM www.wlrfm.com	95.1, 97.5 FM	Co. Waterford